100 LESSONS FOR SUCCESSFUL PROPERTY INVESTING:

The Ultimate Guide to Buy-to-Let in the post-COVID 'New Normal'

By Samantha Latchayya

Property Life
Website: www.property-life.co.uk
Social Media: @Property_Life_

CONTENTS

To my close friends and family. You have more faith in me than I ever have in myself. This book is dedicated to you all. To my husband, well done for putting up with this – I love you!

To my Property Life followers on Instagram, this book has been written especially with you all in mind. Thank you for your support, encouragement and input over the last two years. The property community really is a wonderful thing to be a part of.

INTRODUCTION

Welcome to **100 Lessons for Successful Property Investing:** *The Ultimate Guide to Buy-to-Let in the post-COVID 'New Normal'*. Within this book you will find absolutely everything you need to know about buy-to-let investments broken down into 100 easily digestible lessons. Through the application of the strategies and methods presented in this book, you will be well equipped to confidently create your own successful property portfolio that could generate a stable income for you.

Property investment has been creating wealth for many of the world's most successful people for hundreds of years. Many of the richest people on the planet have made their wealth through property and are continuing to do so today[1]. However, many people still shy away from it, considering it risky, complicated and/or overwhelming. Despite the housing market increasing in value significantly and predictably for decades, the majority of people will still choose a 9-5 job, working hard to earn a mediocre income which they are then programmed to spend quickly whilst impatiently waiting for the next payday. These people will work hard for many years, only to receive a pension that will barely cover day to day essentials.

The truth is that property investment is actually incredibly easy to succeed in. The market can be analysed using research methods, so that sound investments can be made with confidence. Throughout this book, you will learn how investing money in property can actually be safer and wiser than leaving it in the bank. You will be provided with all the required tools and skill set to accurately analyse the property market, research areas of interest and make sound purchases that yield excellent financial returns through tenanting and capital gains.

This book has been written and published in the post-COVID world, where adjusting to the so called 'New Normal' has been essential. The property market has been considerably affected due to the pandemic, with investing and tenanting norms changing almost overnight. This book has everything covered and takes into consideration all the essential adjustments required due to COVID.

How to read this book:

This book is split into the following four sections to consider the chronological order of making a buy-to-let purchase:

-   **Phase 1: Planning your Journey**
-   **Phase 2: Choosing Investments**
-   **Phase 3: Purchasing Property**
-   **Phase 4: Tenanting & Beyond**

The 100 lessons for successful property investing have been carefully grouped into four parts and further categorised into fifteen chapters. This book has been structured in this way so that you can choose to read it all at once, or you can pick it up and learn 'on the go' as you proceed with your investment journey. You can also flick back to different chapters as you repeat the process to grow your portfolio. Those with busy schedules may prefer to tackle one lesson per day, which would make you property smart in a little over three months.

Depending on the complexity of the lessons, some are shorter or longer than others. However, each lesson covers everything you need to know, in a simple and straightforward manner. To ensure that the book's content remains accurate over time, lots of time sensitive data is omitted. Rather than spoon-feed you today's numbers, this book will teach you how to analyse the market so that you are always ahead of the game.

Occasionally, lessons tie into each other as topics are examined in more detail. Box brackets will indicate the lesson number should you wish to flick back or skip ahead to read up on that specific topic in more detail.

In addition to the 100 lessons, this book also includes the **ten things you should NOT do in property investment**, the **50 Questions for Viewings** template, a full breakdown of the **THESIS © research method** and a comprehensive **property glossary**.

To take your property education further, follow Property Life on Instagram (@Property_Life_) for free tips and inspiration.

You can also visit www.property-life.co.uk where you will find plenty of free downloadable resources, be able to sign up for a Property Life Circle © and access several useful tools (such as budgeting and financing spreadsheets and checklists), or sign up for a 1-2-1 property consultation with Samantha Latchayya herself.

PHASE ONE: PLANNING YOUR JOURNEY

CHAPTER 1: LAYING THE FOUNDATIONS

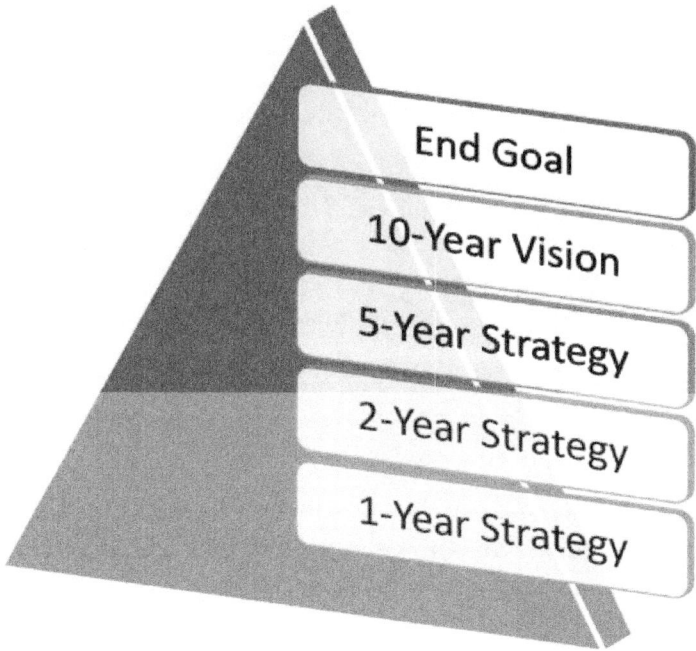

1. START WITH YOUR END GOAL

Why are you investing in property in the first place?

People tend to invest in property for one of two main reasons, depending on their end goal.

1. To generate or boost disposable income (i.e. to enhance the quality of everyday life, break away from a 9-5 job and afford luxuries such as holidays) – instant gratification.
2. To boost long-term savings (i.e. to replace an insufficient pension pot or aid with early retirement) – deferred gratification.

In property investment, you will find that there are many people looking to quit the 9-5 working life commonly known as the 'rat race' by generating enough income through property investment to fund a comfortable life through, earning money in the form of rental returns rather than a salary from an employer.

Equally, there are many people who are happy in their current situations but want to set themselves up financially in the long-term by investing in property.

Whichever category you fall into, it's essential to define your end goal at the very start of your property investment journey. This is because every single investment decision you make should directly reflect this end goal.

If your end goal is to secure a stable income for yourself each month, your focus should be on sourcing rental properties which provide high yields [39]. You must source properties that tick all the THESIS © boxes [35] and will be attractive to tenants. The property may not increase in value beyond inflation over time, but it will provide a steady and reliable income for years to come.

Those whose end goal is to use property investment as a retirement strategy should be less concerned with yields and more focussed on long-term capital growth by investing in properties which are most likely to increase in market value significantly overtime. This could be in regeneration or development areas, found by researching government and council websites to discover where future growth is likely to be.

Of course, if you can achieve high yields *and* long-term growth in one property, you are on to a real winner. But it is still incredibly important that you define your end goal and that every decision you make will take you closer to achieving it.

To help you come up with your end goal, try these two simple techniques.

1. Come up with a 10-year vision

Try to imagine where you would like your life to be in 10 years. What do you want to have achieved (qualifications, promotions, financial freedom...)? What experiences do you want to have had (wedding, family, travel...)? How many properties would you like to own and how much income would you like to achieve per annum? We choose to look a whole decade ahead as it is easy to think big and be as ambitious as we dare. Write everything down on paper as a list or spider diagram – whatever will help you visualise your future the easiest – and be as detailed as possible.

2. Practice asking yourself why

Start by asking why you want to invest in property. Now, keep on asking yourself 'why' as many times as you can. This approach forces you to elaborate on your reasonings and can help you to delve further into the meaning behind your first answer.

The exercise could go something like this:

Why do I want to invest in property?
Because I want to earn more money every month.
Why?
So that I can quit my job.
Why?
Because I'm unhappy in the rat-race and want to work under my own terms.
Why?
So that I have the freedom to travel and spend more time with my family.

By setting your end goal at the beginning of your investment journey, you are ensuring that you constantly have a target to aim towards and something to measure your success against. A well-defined end goal will set you up for long-term success by acting as a guide that will keep you on the right path to achieving everything you want.

2. KNOW YOUR FINANCIALLY FREE NUMBER

Your financially free number is the amount of money you need to earn per annum, in order to live your desired life without needing to work for it. It is achieved by making money work hard, rather than working hard for money. Property investing is one avenue to financial freedom, since the money you invest into property works hard for you and creates more money through returns on investment.

Ask yourself this: In order to be financially free, and live happily on the profits of your investments without needing to work hard for money, how much income would you need to generate?

To calculate this, work out the annual cost of your target lifestyle. This must account for all essential bills, general spending and leisure activities such as socialising and holiday funds. Make sure to also account for savings so that you can keep expanding your portfolio. If your financially free life includes a nice car or any other luxuries such as holidays, fancy dinners and expensive Christmas gifts, you'll need to account for the cost of those, too. Be as detailed as possible, budgeting for absolutely everything you expect to spend in a typical year. Finally, add on at least a 10% buffer to account for any unexpected costs or things you might have forgotten. Divide your annual cost of living by 12 to get your required monthly income after tax.

You can take this one step further by predicting around how many rental properties you will need to own in order to achieve your financially free number. Even though this won't be entirely accurate and can change overtime depending on the market, it will give you a good indication of how many investments you need to aim towards, and you can build in this number when it comes to creating your strategies.

To calculate the approximate number of properties required, do a little research to determine the average profit you can expect to receive from each property (using current mortgage rates, property prices, agency fees, rental fees, taxation, etc.). Then, divide your financially free number by your average profit per property to get your answer. You might be pleasantly surprised at the number of investments you need to live your dream life!

For instance, if my financially free number is £40,000 after tax per year (£3333.33/month), and I expect to earn £400 profit from each property, I would require 9 properties in my portfolio.

You can work out this number based on your dream lifestyle but also on your current income. If something were to happen and your current income source was taken away, how many properties would you need under your belt to match that income?

Now that you know your financially free number and have an idea of how many properties you need to achieve it, you're ready to build your 1, 2 & 5-year strategies to make it a reality.

3. CREATE 1, 2 AND 5-YEAR STRATEGIES

Setting your 1, 2 and 5-year strategies in line with your end goal and 10-year vision is extremely important, and you should spend a significant amount of time drawing these up as accurately and as detailed as possible. The most successful businesses take weeks - sometimes even months - to come up with successful strategies, and your investment plans are just as important.

Using your 10-year vision [1], write down which elements of this you believe you can realistically achieve over the next five years. Next, decide what you will aim to achieve in the first and second year, starting from today. Finally, (and most importantly) break down the first year into monthly segments, listing exactly what you aim to achieve each month. This should include a monthly savings goal and small steps you will take to ensure that you move closer towards achieving your strategies. The more you break down your strategies, the easier they are to achieve and the more realistic they will seem.

You might find that the first two years seem relatively boring compared to your 5-year strategy, 10-year vision and end goal. But as your returns on investment increase and your portfolio grows, it will become more and more exciting. Depending on where you currently are on your property journey, you may require the first couple of years to save up and lay foundations. Don't let this put you off, as your future self will thank you later for the time spent doing the groundwork now.

Remember, the snowball effect will make it easier to achieve more and more overtime. So if you want to own ten properties in five years, it would be unrealistic to say you will buy two properties every year, and more realistic to say that you will buy one property each in years one and two, two properties each in years three and four, and four properties in year five.

Finally, ensure that all your strategies are SMART: **S**pecific, **M**easurable, **A**chievable, **R**ealistic and **T**imed, and don't forget to take the 18-year property cycle [23] into consideration when planning your goals and strategies as you will need to take different actions depending on what market you will be dealing with.

4. TELL PEOPLE YOUR PLANS BUT NOT YOUR IDEAS

In other words, tell people what your intentions are, but don't tell them how you plan to achieve them. Tell them your end goal, but keep your 1, 2 and 5-year strategies to yourself.

Why? Well, saying your end goal out loud makes you more determined to achieve it. It tells people you're serious and makes it more 'real'. But telling people your ideas - going into detail - can result in you being given advice by people who may not be as clued up as you.

Those who have your best interests at heart but aren't necessarily as switched on as you are when it comes to property investing, may view your ideas as risky or unrealistic and encourage you to follow their tried and tested paths. This can be discouraging and confusing.

For instance, if you tell a close network of friends that you intend to become a professional, self-employed property developer over the next 20 years or so, you will appear ambitious and confident. However, if you explain that you plan to get rid of your fancy car and buy a run-down terraced house in a regeneration area using an interest-only mortgage, you might see your friends' faces drop slightly and the unsolicited advice will begin to roll in. This does not mean that your idea is not brilliant, but it may mean that those around you don't quite understand the ins and outs of your strategies and might worry on your behalf - even though they don't need to.

Whilst it can be exciting to tell friends and family about your property intentions and you may want to share your success stories with them, be cautious as to how much information you share and even more cautious as to how much advice you accept once the topic is brought up.

Finally, as the market changes and different opportunities arise, your strategies should change in line with them. Yet, whilst your short-term actions may change, your end goal will remain the same. By telling people your plans but not your ideas, you can get support from those around you, without allowing people to pass judgement on your short-term success.

5. EAT THE ELEPHANT

For those who are not sure how to get started and find taking the first step daunting, consider the 'eat the elephant' approach. The theory behind this technique is that you of course could not eat an entire elephant in one sitting. Yet, if you broke it down into tiny pieces, you could eventually eat the whole elephant, one piece at a time. A strange analogy, yes - but trust me, it works!

With investing, you should always consider breaking your investment goals into 'edible bites'. This is particularly important with your 1-year strategy. Consider one task, such as purchasing a single property, and break that down into as many small steps as possible. Now work on 'eating' one 'piece' at a time and you'll be surprised at how quickly you 'eat the whole elephant'.

For the more experienced investor, it is completely normal to have more than one 'elephant' on the go at all times.

This strategy is a useful visual aid to ensure you are constantly progressing and to help you realise how a task that seems daunting at first can be easily digested.

When you try this technique, you can choose to draw it out in whichever way is easiest for you. I've seen people draw actual elephants and divide it up into sections, with one task inside each part of the animal. But you can also use a simple pie chart, Gantt chart, spider diagram or a plain old list to extrapolate the steps. Once you have listed all the small elements that make up the larger task, order them and consider adding deadlines to help you make your way through to the end.

How do you eat an elephant? One piece at a time.

6. CONSTANTLY RE-EVALUATE YOUR STRATEGIES

When it comes to property investment, everything can change in a matter of days (new government policies, a change in personal circumstances, unexpected opportunities, global pandemics, and so forth). To that end, it is important to always re-evaluate your strategies.

It is fundamental that you are always working towards strategies. Yet, it is equally important to allow these strategies to be fluid and adapt over time.

As you work through your 1-year strategy (which you have broken down into monthly segments), constantly evaluate your progress to make sure that you are on track. Your 1-year strategy should be so well researched and broken down that you are able to easily stay on track. However, it is not unusual to experience an unexpected hurdle or, if you're lucky, to move forward quicker than anticipated. Whatever the case, constantly assess your position in line with your strategies and personal targets. Wherever necessary, tweak your strategies in line with your progress and changes in the market. This will ensure that you are always working towards the best possible outcomes.

You should look to re-evaluate your 1-year strategy each month and consider your 2 and 5-year strategies at least every quarter, making as many adaptations as required. The objective is not to set strategies on day one, and five years later make some more. Rather, it's more like playing a long game of chess - always thinking several steps ahead and readjusting your strategy depending on what moves have already been played.

As well as your strategies, make sure that you also re-evaluate your existing investments, calculating the true return on investments (ROIs) and yields in line with market changes. When applicable, review your mortgages and other products/services to ensure that the deals/tariffs you have are still competitive.

This is a step that absolutely cannot be avoided. Set aside time every month and every quarter in your calendar to sit down to re-evaluate your strategies and current properties. As Abraham Lincoln so perfectly put it:

"Give me six hours to chop down a tree, and I will spend the first four sharpening the axe".

CHAPTER 2: MANAGING YOUR MONEY

7. GET YOUR MONEY IN ORDER

Before you can even think about buying property, you must know your financial position inside-out and have a strong idea on how your savings will develop in the short and long-term.

You may have money already set aside for your first/next investment, be about to start saving for the first time, or perhaps you have debt that you must clear before you can start saving. Whatever your situation, having your finances in order will help maximise success.

If you don't know the exact breakdown of your financial situation, you are at risk of starting off on the wrong foot.

Here are three steps you should take to get your finances in order.

1. **Create a finance spreadsheet**

This should list all your incomings and outgoings each month, from mortgage payments and bills, to food and social budgets. The spreadsheet should also include a column for savings, which should be considered as a cost and must be budgeted for.

Once you have listed every single cost, see if you can reduce any of them. Perhaps your food budget could be cut if you got less takeaways, or maybe your bills could be reduced by switching providers. Look for subscription payments that you could live without and consider if luxury items such as holidays and car payments could be reduced by temporarily driving a less expensive car or going on less holidays (or cheaper holidays) whilst you save. By playing around with your spreadsheet you will be surprised to see how small changes can save you significant amounts of money. For instance, those who usually buy a £2.50 hot drink before work every weekday could save over £500 a year by eliminating this non-essential purchase. Those who have experienced working from home recently due to COVID may already have recognised a change in spending habits.

Use your finance spreadsheet to create budgets within each spending category and aim to stick to them. If you have any bad debt [8] create a strategy to pay off a certain amount each month to get you debt free for good.

You should update this spreadsheet at least every month, to track your progress and identify opportunities and weaknesses.

If you would like to download a copy of the pre-formatted Property Life budget calculator, visit www.property-life.co.uk/resources.

2. Obtain an Agreement in Principle (AIP)

Another essential part of getting your finances in order is to make sure that you can borrow the amount you need when you find the right property. Many people wait until they have found the right property to obtain an AIP and get their finances in order. This is how many purchases 'fall through', due to unprepared buyers.

The right way to go about things is to gain your AIP by completing a short online form in advance of your property search. This way, you will know exactly how much money you are able to borrow and have an AIP to show sellers/agencies when you go in with a bid. Shockingly, most people won't do this, so you will stand out for being efficient and prepared. If you apply for an AIP and don't achieve the figure you had hoped for, you will still have time to reconsider your strategy or make changes that will improve your AIP results, before you start making bids. An AIP is normally only valid for 90 days, but you can apply as many times as you like, and it won't affect your credit score [9].

3. Hold your money in the right places

Some of the better bank accounts for building savings can lock up your money for a set time or have processes in place that means it can take longer than usual to access your cash when you need it. To that end, when you are preparing to start the buying process, it is important that you move any money that you will require for a deposit or professional fees into an easy access account.

Equally, if you are saving for the long term, assess whether your money would be best kept in a savings account with a high interest rate. For large amounts of money, a tiny difference in a percentage of interest could make a big difference to your savings. With this in mind, make sure you frequently check that the money you are saving is held in the best possible account as the interest rates that initially draw you into opening an account can quickly dwindle.

Finally, it is wise to keep money allocated for different things in different accounts. For instance, if you have a rental property it is smart to set up a bank account specifically for that property only. This makes it much easier when you need to log your finances or work out tax payments. It's also easier for tracking rental payments and spotting if anything is missing.

8. KNOW YOUR ASSETS FROM YOUR LIABILITIES

Simply put, **assets MAKE money**, and **liabilities TAKE money**.

Assets are things which increase in value and generate capital, ideally periodically, to enhance your income. This includes any type of belongings or investments which will increase in value over time at a higher rate than the cost to own the debt.

Liabilities are items which cost you money to own. They may also depreciate the longer you own them. This includes cars, designer clothes, credit card debt and (some say) even off-spring! – But I'll let you decide that one for yourself.

Both assets and liabilities can be purchased using debt. Depending on what the debt is used for will determine if that debt is 'good' or 'bad'.

Good debt refers to borrowing money in order to invest in assets. Mortgages used for investments are a form of good debt. Investing in property using good debt is called 'leverage' [57]. Bad debt is used to acquire liabilities.

The home that you live in can be considered an asset AND a liability. The most common standpoint by investors is that a home is a liability as it does not generate income and costs money to use (bills, council tax, repairs, etc.). However, as with all property it can appreciate overtime. In this case, the rule of thumb is that whilst a home is being used for your own living arrangements, it is a liability. It would only become an asset at the point of selling or, possibly, remortgaging to release equity for an investment – at which point it would be considered a 'property' rather than a 'home'.

People who describe themselves as being 'tied-down' tend to own too many liabilities which they pay for through an earned income such as a 9-5 job. They also own lots of 'bad debt' to finance a lifestyle which is above their earnings.

In order to become financially free in the future, it may be necessary to sacrifice spending on liabilities whilst you put in a few years of asset building. The more liabilities you own now, the less successful you allow yourself to become in the future.

If you were to make a list of your assets and another of your liabilities, what would your lists look like?

The target should be to generate more capital through assets than you spend on liabilities.

Only once you understand assets, liabilities, good debt and bad debt, can you really start to consciously save, spend and invest money wisely.

9. MAINTAIN GOOD CREDIT

Do you know what your credit score is?

When it comes to applying for a mortgage, one of the first things that a lender will do is run a credit search to discover your financial history and current financial status. If you want to be approved for a mortgage, you must ensure that you have an excellent credit score. Otherwise, your loan application could be declined, and your property journey would be very short-lived indeed.

Your score is calculated by a credit reference agency (CRA) who are sent information by lenders (your credit report). Your score will be based on your credit history and how you've managed your finances in the past. Other information, such as public records (electoral roll, court judgments, etc.) also contribute towards your report. This allows lenders to assess your level of risk when you apply for credit. The higher the number, the better your credit score. The maximum score you can attain depends on which platform is being used.

Building up a good credit score is all about proving that you are a trustworthy and reliable lender. A history of borrowing and paying back loans will help showcase your trustworthiness and increase your score. If you have never had any debt before, you won't have had an opportunity to showcase your ability to pay it back, meaning your credit score will be low.

Maintaining good credit involves a careful balance of obtaining some debt and proving that you can be relied on to pay it off on time. Using a credit card is a great way to build a credit score if you pay back your debt regularly and in full. Taking on a phone contract is another way to show your potential lender that you are a trusted customer. However, if you miss any payments or apply for too much debt, this will reflect negatively on your credit score and make lenders less likely to approve your mortgage application.

When you apply for these kinds of 'debt' the company you are applying with may run a credit search on you to determine for themselves if you would be a reliable customer. Searches can be 'hard' or 'soft'. An AIP (agreement in principle) won't affect your credit score as it's considered a 'soft search'. A hard search such as an application for a phone contract, credit card or mortgage will show up on your credit report as a request to take on debt. If a company wants to run a credit search on you, always find out if it would be a hard or soft search first and think twice if you are about to apply for a mortgage.

It's incredibly easy to keep a check on your credit score free of charge by using credit score apps and websites. There are some chargeable services, but unless your score is disastrous and needs your full attention, you won't need to delve that deep. Services such as Clear Score will show you your score and what you can do to improve it, free of charge. It can take months to build up a good credit score (or years if it is terrible), so don't delay in finding out what yours is.

Even if you think you have a perfect credit score, it's always worth checking if there's something you can do to raise it even higher. You should also check regularly that there are no mistakes on your report. If you do notice any errors, you must appeal to get them rectified which can take a long time.

10. PAY YOURSELF FIRST

Often, the main hurdle for purchasing property will be capital. In order to buy a property, you will need money for a deposit plus a few extra thousand pounds for solicitors, stamp duty and everything in between. The good news is that it's easy to save quickly, and unless you work for Money Saving Expert, I'm confident that there will be at least one small change you can make to improve your savings each month.

The easiest and most effective way to save quickly is by paying yourself first. This means that whenever you receive money, whether it be from a salary, property or side hustle, you should immediately put aside a set amount into a savings account.

The biggest mistake people can make when it comes to saving money is to spend first and then save whatever is left-over at the end. This is because people are programmed to 'live to their means' no matter how much they earn. Especially nowadays with contactless payments and 'one-click' online purchases, it's easier than ever for people to spend much more than they realise. Often, they will spend all their money just before pay-day and then count down the days until their bank account is topped up. Those who leave saving to the end of the month will find more often than not they have very little money left to put into a savings account.

As soon as you receive an income, whether it be a wage from a 9-5 job, rental income or anything in between, pay yourself first. Understand your financial situation inside-out and set up standing orders that will transfer money into savings accounts as soon as the money comes in. The amount you save should be worked out by taking into consideration all your outgoings and based on a budget you set yourself. Don't make day-to-day life difficult by saving too much - but do save as much as you realistically can.

If you have any bad debt [8], a contribution towards paying it off should be the first payment you make. Only once you have paid yourself to cover your savings and any bad debt repayments, should you allow yourself to spend what is left.

Remember that life isn't only about saving money and it's OK to spend, too. Once you have 'paid yourself first', contributing to your savings and enhancing your future, be sure to enjoy the rest of the month, using the money you allocated for spending guilt-free.

11. IT IS POSSIBLE TO BUY PROPERTY WITH NO MONEY OF YOUR OWN

Yes. It is possible to purchase property without having plenty of your own cash saved up. This is commonly referred to as OPM (Other People's Money).

Here are four OPM strategies that can help you invest in property without the need to use any of your own capital.

1. Angel Investors

Usually a private, individual investor who agrees to provide financial backing for an investment in exchange for a return on the profits or agreed inflated repayment after a set term. An angel investor will lend in order to enhance the value of their own money, as they can usually expect to make between 10-20% of their investment back over a short period, which is more lucrative than if they were to keep it in a bank account. An angel investor can also be a friend or family member who lends you money under mutually agreed terms to help you get on the property ladder (sometimes referred to as 'the bank of mum and dad').

2. Bridging Finance

These are short term loans (usually between 1-18 months only) which are provided by a bridging company. There are usually no monthly repayments - just one set date that the entire loan must be repaid in full, plus interest.

Bridge to let loans are aimed specifically at the buy-to-let market. The fixed term loan is used to secure a property in place of a mortgage. Before the end of the loan's fixed term, you should aim to refinance into a standard buy-to-let mortgage and pay of the bridging loan in full.

3. **Peer to Peer (P2P) lending:**

P2P lending occurs between a lender (someone with a cash reserve who wants to lend as a form of investment) and a borrower (in this case the property investor). The transaction usually takes place via a professional P2P lending website. The lender will deposit their chosen amount of money into the P2P company and stipulate what type of interest they want to charge and when they want their money back. The investor uses the P2P platform to apply for the loan and must agree to the lending terms. Until recently, this was considered quite risky. However, over the last few years, professional P2P companies have proven to be both safe and lucrative for lenders and borrowers alike, making them a viable option for quick funding.

4. **Credit Cards**

In some cases, it is possible to use a credit card (or overdraft) for a property deposit. This is by no means as simple as handing over your credit card and inputting your pin code to pay for a deposit – that's a big no-no! But in some instances, you can access capital from a credit card to go towards a property purchase, for instance though a 0% money transfer. Many lenders do not support deposits which come from debt such as a loan or credit card, so this is not always an option. But each lender will have a different method for assessing your debt to income ratio and risk as a borrower. Whilst many lenders insist that a deposit comes from your own existing, saved capital, some lenders may be willing to accept money attained from a money transfer to count towards your deposit. This largely depends on the conditions of the market and the lenders' willingness to hand out loans.

Pros of using OPM:

- **Get on the property ladder faster**: Without the need to save up each month, OPM can provide instant capital that can cover all fees and deposits, to fast-track your buying process. In the case of bridging finance, it usually takes around 14 days from application to receiving the money which is much faster than securing a standard mortgage product.

- **Access to more deals**: As you can access capital quickly, you can take advantage of offers that require quick action, such as lucrative off-plan purchases that sell incredibly quickly and auction purchases that require an immediate payment.

Cons of using OPM:

- **Changing lender conditions:** Not all lenders accept money from angel investors as deposits as they may require you to prove you can save and manage money yourself. After the pandemic broke out, some lenders that previously accepted money gifted from parents as deposit contributions retracted their offers as the risk was considered greater and they required further evidence that the investor was reliable.

- **OPM equals debt:** Many mortgage companies dislike credit card debt and therefore won't want to lend to you if they can see your deposit has come from there.

- **Higher interest rates:** As the process holds a higher risk for lenders, the interest rates can be much higher than a standard mortgage. This must be taken into consideration when working out if this strategy would be financially viable.

- **Higher risk**: Often, the strategy to pay back OPM

debt is to increase the value of the property which was purchased by undertaking refurbishments and then re-mortgaging to release equity. However, if for any reason you are not able to release equity (i.e. if the value did not increase enough), it could land you in hot water with re-possession being a likely consequence.

If you do choose to use OPM as a financing strategy, ensure you have a solid plan and consider talking it through with the property community or a financial advisor before proceeding. If you're not 100% confident about the repayments, don't do it! Finally, the terms and conditions are always changing for OPM, meaning its appeal can differ depending on what mortgage providers will accept at the time and how the market is performing. Always consider all options carefully and only use OPM if the deal is right and you don't have access to your own capital.

12. DON'T WORK FOR MONEY - MAKE MONEY WORK FOR YOU

Ellen Goodman, an American journalist and speaker, once said:

"Normal is getting dressed in clothes that you buy for work and driving through traffic in a car that you are still paying for, in order to get to the job you need, to pay for the clothes and the car, and the house you leave vacant all day so you can afford to live in it."

Read this again... and again, until it really sinks in!

Society believes that in order to be successful we must work hard, attend established educational institutions and get good grades so that we can secure a 'safe' 9-5 job and build a career that will pay for the nice lifestyle that marketing moguls lead us to believe we not only want, but need. We are made to believe that the game of life involves a stable job, usually for five out of every seven days of our lives. Once we have the job, we need a mortgage on a large home, a nice car, a nuclear family and lots of belongings. Happiness is quickly reduced to keeping up with The Jones' (or the Kardashians as it now seems) and making money so that it can immediately be spent on depreciating liabilities.

And what is given in return for this 'success'? 5 days a week used up making our employers richer, heaps of stress and such a strong desire to earn more and spend more that we never really achieve true happiness. As soon as we achieve one thing (a degree, a spouse, a career…), we move onto the next objective. 'I'll finally be happy once I have a promotion… a big holiday… another child… a bigger home… a better car… the new iPhone…'.

This really is normal for 95% of people. But if you want to be in the top 5%, you need to escape normal. Rather than working to make money, find a way to make money work for you!

In other words, invest in assets that will create capital overtime, and are not directly related to the amount of work you do.

Every day that you own property which is rented to tenants, your invested money is working for you by putting money straight into your bank account in the form of rent. This money allows you to save up and reinvest into additional properties, resulting in even more money working for you (the snowball effect).

Not only that, but your original money is also working hard via inflation, causing your assets to appreciate, and your debt to depreciate [27].

Property investment allows money to work for you so that you don't have to be 'normal' and work for money.

13. TAKE CONTROL OF YOUR PENSION

Note: This lesson aims to cover the fundamental aspects of the pension crisis to give you an overall understanding of the matter. If you would like to delve further into this topic there are some great materials available online, produced by experts in finance and economics.

Most people have no idea how much money they will need to live well during their retirement and just as many have no idea how much they have in their own pension pots.

Take the time to find out how much you currently have, and how much you ideally need to receive each month to live comfortably. Unfortunately, the majority of people who have worked hard for decades will only receive a fraction of what they would ideally like to, and risk spending the last few decades of life sat at home spending cautiously and worrying about bills.

Currently, the UK government has an auto-enrolment pension scheme with everyone in employment contributing each month. But the fact is that nobody is really saving enough for the amount of years they will be alive post-retirement.

Terrifyingly, there is almost complete certainty that a pension crisis is looming. This means that those of us who will be approaching retirement age over the next two or more decades are likely to experience a total failing of the state pension as we currently know it.

What is the pension crisis?

Simply put, the pension crisis, also referred to as the pension time bomb, is the prediction that over the next few decades, it is inevitable that government retirement funds will be insufficient to pay the pensions of those who will require them. There simply will not be enough money saved up by prior generations, to pay out enough money to those who have contributed to it for so many years.

Three causes of the pension crisis:

1. **People are living longer**: State pensions were introduced in the UK in 1948, when life expectancy was much lower than it is today - so a pension didn't have to pay out for as long. Nowadays, as people live longer, pension pots are stretched over larger periods of time. As a result, many of us who have at least two decades of work until retirement face the threat that our pensions might not actually be available to us by the time we reach retirement age, due to overdemand.

2. **People aren't saving enough**: As of 2020 the most you can get from a basic state pension after years of working, is a meagre £134.25 per week[2], which certainly won't fund anything exciting as you try to enjoy the final years of your life. Although it is possible to access a private pension if you have added to a private pot, the reality is that many people aren't aware of their options. It has been found that one in three people are relying solely on the state to fund their retirement and they will only receive the full amount if they have made sufficient contributions[3]. Furthermore, those who are self-employed do not get auto enrolled onto a pension so may not be contributing at all.

3. **There is a lower ratio of workers per retiree:** The working generation's National Insurance pays the retired generation's pensions[4]. As the number of

people who are retired becomes larger than the number of contributors, existing taxpayers must support a greater amount of retired people.

There's ages until I retire, surely the government will sort it out by then?

Yes, there could be a miracle pension reform which prevents the pension crisis. However, at this stage it is quite unlikely and certainly not worth the risk of sitting back to see what happens. If you want to enjoy your retirement without living to a strict budget and worrying about the crisis, you need to take responsibility of your own financial affairs.

In fact, the longer you have until you reach retirement age, the more at risk you are of becoming a victim of the pension crisis.

Additionally, as people live longer, the official retirement age set by the government continues to increase. In 2018 this age was 65 for men and women. By 2040, the government currently estimates that they will raise the state pension age to 69 for everyone (but this could be higher as recent years have seen the government speed up new pension age reforms)[5]. I don't know about you, but I don't want to be working throughout my 60s!

What can I do about this?

The smartest thing to do would be to seek an alternative way to relying solely on a pension. This is not to say that you should stop contributing towards a pension, but you should avoid keeping all your eggs in one basket.

One alternative to relying solely on pension pots to live off during the later years of your life is to use property to grow your own retirement fund.

Consider investing in one property that is a sound, long-term investment. A property which will give you a rental return but, most importantly, is in a great location that is highly likely to grow in value overtime. Name this property your retirement fund. Each month save all or as much of the profit as you can to act as your own pension contribution. You may choose to re-invest these savings into more property, lock it up in a lucrative savings account, or do a combination of both. Allow property to grow your wealth and your pension pot, keeping the guarantee in your own hands. When you decide you want to retire, you can access your property retirement fund, or choose to sell some of the property you bought as assets to fund the last decades of your life.

If you have already worked for a number of years and have a good chunk of pension money built up, consider accessing a percentage of it now to invest in property. The government is always changing the legislation surrounding pensions, but it is usually possible to access your pension early (and tax free!). Investing part of your pension money into property will mean that the money still belongs to you, but it is no longer tied up in a pension scheme and can appreciate along with the property market whilst potentially also giving you a rental income.

Remember, just one good property purchase could provide you with more income per month than the government pension that you've contributed to for decades.

CHAPTER 3:
BUILDING AN
EDUCATION BASE

14. LEARN AS YOU GO

When it comes to property investment, not only is it never too late to start... it is also never too early.

It is of course wise to ensure you have a good level of property knowledge before you set out on an investment journey - this is exactly what this book will equip you with. However, what you will find is that through practical application of the knowledge you already have, you will also gain confidence in navigating the industry and learn as you go.

Some people never make the step into property investment because they don't feel they know enough to get started. As the market constantly evolves, policies change and new trends encroach the market, this makes it impossible for these people to ever feel 100% ready, and their property journey never gets off the ground. If we all wait until we know absolutely everything there is to know about property investment, no one would ever get started.

Whilst this book provides you with all the essential knowledge you need to know before setting out into the world of property investment, there will always be more to learn. For instance, when you buy a property you may need to renovate it before you can tenant it. This may involve certain DIY tasks which you haven't done before. You may come across certain obstacles that you haven't faced before or didn't anticipate. This is the nature of property investment and in order to be successful you must be flexible and maintain a can-do attitude. This is where you will learn as you go and gain useful new skills and knowledge during the process.

Even the largest property tycoons must continue learning. This industry is always developing – that's what makes it so fun and interesting! Use this book to obtain your essential knowledge base and then get started, being open to learning as you go.

15. LISTEN TO PODCASTS

A brilliant way to learn about property investment, general business management and even personal development is to invest your time into podcasts. Podcasts have really developed over the last decade and are now exceptional learning tools. Furthermore, they are completely free of charge and can be listened to on the go. This means you can learn whilst you visit potential properties, complete a refurbishment, get on top of your property admin, take a drive around an area of interest or even go for a jog.

As podcasts are released frequently, they provide you with up-to-date information and are more objective than listening to a news channel which will usually summarise a situation as quickly as possible and enhance stories to appear more 'intense' or 'attractive'. Podcasts don't care about scaremongering or click-bait and are often led by professionals who are specialists in their field.

Whilst there are many excellent podcasts out there which are specifically focussed on property investing, there are also some great business podcasts which can be equally as useful for building a successful property portfolio. Ultimately, property investors require many different skills, such as marketing, decorating, DIY, management skills, standard business skills, communication skills and risk management amongst many other things. Listening to podcasts on these topics can boost your knowledge in these areas for free.

Three excellent podcasts that I listen to:

1. **Power Hour**, hosted by Adrienne Herbert, for motivation on achieving success and making the most of the most of your time.
2. **Property Magic Podcast**, for interesting debates on all things property related.
3. **TED Talks Daily**, for thought provoking ideas on every subject imaginable.

Check out www.property-life.co.uk/recommendations for the most up to date list of excellent podcasts which will help enhance your success and your life.

16. AVOID PROPERTY TRAINING COURSES

There are many face-to-face and online training courses that promise to show you how to transform your life through property investment.

The most common property training companies usually start by offering free 1-day events. These are actually marketing talks which are designed to convince you to join a paid course about becoming financially free.

But let's be realistic for a moment – if these courses really could bring you financial freedom, then why aren't the promotors and speakers sat on a private island sipping a mojito right now? Why are the people who hold the so-called secret to financial freedom handing out flyers and hosting seminars in hotel meeting rooms?

The answer is because the courses are simply created to generate income from ticket sales and are not run in your best interest. The people who run these events are some of the best sales professionals in the UK working on commission. They are excellent at their job and know exactly what to say to entice you in. Some of these courses cost as much as an actual property deposit which is absurd. Don't throw away your savings on anything other than safe investments.

Unfortunately, there are dozens of schemes like this out there organised by huge companies. Here are some of the techniques to watch out for and avoid like the plague:

- Using famous property moguls' faces and names on marketing material.

- Offering incentives like freebies when you sign up.
- Limiting the number of people who can sign up to make it look more exclusive (but not telling you the number it's limited to - it could be a million!).
- Not allowing anyone to ask questions during a two-hour pitch so that the speaker can't be challenged.
- Showing you photographs of a luxurious lifestyle and claiming it as their own. Explaining that they achieved this by attending this course 'just like you'.
- Selling the course at an increased price only to slash it right at the end to make people panic buy (just like Black Friday).
- Psychologically challenging you by using terms like 'Most of you probably won't go on this course because you'll be scared' or 'Only the most intelligent people in the room will sign up'.
- Not telling you what is included in the course because it is 'top secret' (in reality it lacks content and would put you off).
- Spoon-feeding you information on how it is possible to become financially free using other people's money. (Which is very high risk [11] and is quite immoral of them to say to a room full of new investors with little prior knowledge).
- The paid course (should you attend) will drip-feed you some obvious knowledge but mostly just try and get you to go on the super expensive 'advanced' course. And 'hey, you've come this far, it would be stupid of you to stop now'.
- They accept credit cards... Well if this isn't the final warning sign, I don't know what is.

If you really want to learn about property investment, you can find everything you need to know IN THIS BOOK and enhance your knowledge by networking with other investors and by learning as you go.

17. TV SHOWS ABOUT PROPERTY ARE NOT EDUCATIONAL TOOLS

You wouldn't watch ER and then think you were qualified to be a doctor. Or watch a few episodes of Law and Order and start to do your own legal work (I hope!). So equally, you shouldn't watch a property series and think you're ready to embark on an investment project.

Nowadays, there are so many different property shows on TV that are successful in the same way as property courses. They lead you to believe that property investing is a simple, fool-proof way to make quick money. Whilst they can be interesting and fun to watch, make sure that you take them with a pinch of salt and remember that they are reality shows, edited for entertainment and certainly not educational programs.

Of course, these 30-60-minute programmes can only show you the highlights of an investment journey, which will usually include the rewards, the super highs and the super lows. What you won't see is an accurate breakdown of the yields or ROI, all the sleepless nights and hard graft.

There simply isn't enough time in a show that speeds you

through several different people's renovation projects, to go into enough detail to give you the full picture. And if the program really went into as much detail as is required for an investment project, it just would not be as exciting, and the show would not get as many viewers.

By all means, do enjoy these programmes about buying a home abroad, purchasing through auction, renovating farm houses and building your own 10-bedroom castle out of fiberglass and pennies; but always bear in mind that a property education will not be gained by sitting on the sofa watching TV.

18. NETWORK

Networking is fundamental for any business and property is no exception. The more you network, the more you learn and the more you hear about new opportunities.

Through networking, property investors can discuss the latest market updates, problem solve each other's challenges and support and motivate each other. Through simple conversations about a shared passion, you could find yourself talking to investors who have different approaches to you or access to different location knowledge that you might find very useful. There is plenty of property out there for everyone and each investor is following different strategies to attain their own end goals. Don't be afraid to share your own learnings and experiences as what you will gain in return will be priceless.

Consider these three quotes and what they mean in terms of successful networking strategies:

1. **"If you're the smartest person in the room, you're in the wrong room."**

Attend face-to-face or online property mixers, conferences and meetups. You may have to pay to attend, but they will include important talks from keynote speakers and guarantee you a space full of likeminded investors all looking to meet new people. There are also forums full of investors looking to chat about ideas, strategies and all things property.

2. **"It's not what you know, it's who you know."**

Set time aside every quarter or so, to network with your estate agents, brokers and financial advisors. Regularly touching base with these professionals could lead to invaluable insight that gives you an edge over other investors. For instance, an agent could let you know about a property that is about to go to market in your preferred location, or your broker may tell you about a new mortgage incentive being released. Keep in touch with your professionals and they may remember you when they hear something exciting.

3. **"Surround yourself with the people you want to become."**

Follow the social media accounts of successful investors and comment on their posts. Those who use platforms such as Instagram are likely to be open to meeting new people and chatting about property. This is a free and fast way to connect with other investors.

Other useful networking strategies:

- Send holiday cards to your professional contacts. Keeping your name and friendly nature at the forefront of their mind will help give you an edge over their other clients.
- Discuss your end goals with friends, family and associates so that they think of you if they hear of a good opportunity, such as a colleague of theirs looking for a quick sale [4].
- **Join a Property Life Circle** © [19].

What's unique about property investing professionals is that unlike many other professional sectors, the competition is much less aggressive, and individuals are much more willing to get together and share experiences. Those who put themselves out there and get to know other property investors are much more likely to succeed as they have access to a greater amount of ideas, recommendations, professional opinions, support networks and contacts.

19. JOIN A PROPERTY LIFE CIRCLE ©

Networking is an excellent way to learn more about investing. The property industry is full of amazing people who are happy to share their experiences and learn from one another. Property Life Circles facilitate networking by bringing investors together and encouraging development.

What exactly are Property Life Circles ©?

Property Life Circles © is a concept developed by Property Life, which brings together small to medium-sized groups of like-minded investors to act as a close power unit and support system. Property Life provides the foundations for likeminded professionals to come together and expand their professional network, meeting other investors within the industry. Each circle connects between 3 - 8 investors who are on similar property journeys.

Through your Property Life Circle, you will access each other's information and be encouraged to meet up either in person (when possible) or virtually at least once per quarter in order to chat about all things property related. This can include sharing details of your progress, outlining your goals and discussing different investment strategies, locations and more. By proactively choosing to surround yourself with a community of ambitious professionals at least four times per year, you will present yourself with the opportunity to be motivated, inspired and further educated.

Networking with like-minded individuals who all aspire towards the same goals and achievements has proven to be an invaluable tool that I encourage every reader to take advantage of.

To sign up to a Property Life Circle © or learn more about the benefits of joining one, visit www.property-life.co.uk/circles.

20. KEEP AN EYE ON POLITICS

You don't have to be a politics buff to succeed in property. But being in the know when it comes to new policies will definitely work in your favour.

When it comes to politics, it can impact a property investor in two ways.

1. **Directly:** E.g. new policies which landlords must adhere to, changes in legislation, SDLT adjustments, etc.
2. **Indirectly**: E.g. agreeing plans to build new roads or buildings that could potentially adjust the value of an area.

If you really can't stand politics or find it difficult to follow, a simple way to keep up to date with the latest policies that may affect the property market is to follow reputable social media accounts that outline the most important updates for you. Rather than relying solely on the news[6], you can get more accurate information by subscribing to local council newsletters, reading posts by highly esteemed property bloggers and listening to property podcasts. Wherever you seek your political updates from, make sure that they are completely unbiased, reliable and factual.

Additionally, when general elections are held, take the time vote. Many people in the UK don't exercise their right to vote and it is, well... lazy. Take five minutes out of your day to check if you are registered correctly to vote. If you're a busy person or just want the easiest route, you can register for postal voting through your local council.

When considering which party to vote for, ask yourself what is most important to you. Make a point of researching the opinions and promises of each party in terms of property. For instance, what does the party propose regarding stamp duty and rental regulations? Have any parties pledged to build more houses to tackle the housing crisis? Are the parties working with or against landlords? Perhaps they propose more legislation which would make an investor's job more difficult or, alternatively, make it a little easier.

I am definitely not suggesting that property policies should be the only deciding factor in where you pledge your vote, as there are many important things that the government needs to tackle. But you should ensure that you understand the stance of each party when the time comes to decide who you want to give your vote to.

21. NATIONAL STATISTICS ARE COMPLETELY USELESS

National statistics are prepared to measure and compare the performance of different economies. The media will often publish these to summarise the performance of a market. But you won't only see national statistics relating to property in the news, as leading property researchers will also use them. National statistics consider numbers taken from across the nation to calculate the average. This figure is used to summarise the whole market. National statistics can be (slightly) useful when considered over a long period of time, for example to measure how property prices have increased over 50 years, or how interest rates have fluctuated since 1920. Yet, considered alone, or over a short period of time, they are truly useless.

This is because the sample of information that is being summarised is far too large for it to be helpful in understanding the property industry or identifying patterns.

To illustrate how useless national statistics can be when used within the context of property investment, imagine over a five-year period that house prices in the South of England have increased by 10%. Now imagine house prices in the North of England experienced a 10% decline. If only the national statistics were considered, it would report that nothing had changed nationally[7].

National statistics do not provide useful information when it comes to maintaining your property knowledge and education. More often than not, you will only find them used in the media to create propaganda and click bait. The best way to keep informed on property market movements is to do your own research using the ample information available online through government web pages or through highly esteemed organisations such as property associations [87].

22. READ BETWEEN
THE LINES

When was the last time you saw a headline on the front of a newspaper that was reporting good news? The truth is the media will always favour bad news over good as it sells better.

This is no different when it comes to the property market. Should you only get your property updates from news articles, you would be forgiven for thinking that property investment was a terrible idea full of risk. Just type 'property market news' into a search engine and you can bet that most of the headlines will be gloomy and pessimistic.

This is because the majority of the time, 'news' is a regurgitated fact which has been reworded and enhanced in order to catch the eye of the reader or listener. All news corporations are businesses seeking to make a profit, and bad news sells more papers. Headlines work in the same way as 'clickbait' which are one-liners taken out of context to capture the interest of as many people as possible without necessarily focussing on what is accurate, but rather what will cause the audience to feel the need to read/listen further. The media is also responsible for a lot of propaganda (misleading or biased information that is used to promote a political cause or specific point of view that is not necessarily accurate) and different news companies have different political agendas.

To combat this, it is essential to learn to read between the lines. If the media releases a scary statistic, consider where they got their facts from. What time period is it based on and what data did they use? Who are they using for quotes and references? Finally, ask yourself who the target market is. If it is not written specifically for the professional investor, reconsider if this is a reliable or useful source.

Even better than learning to read between the lines is to actively cut out the media from your property education (I recommend you do this immediately). Be sure to replace it with new, reliable sources of information to ensure that you are always in the know. This can include property specific podcasts, property magazines, property associations and investor networking opportunities.

CHAPTER 4: THE PROPERTY MARKET

23. KNOW WHERE YOU ARE IN THE 18-YEAR PROPERTY CYCLE

The 18-year property cycle is one of the most important concepts to understand if you are to succeed in property investment.

Simply put, the 18-year property cycle is based on the theory that the property market completes a 4-stage cycle every 18 years. Each stage is a consequence of the previous stage, the fourth causing the first to start over again. The cycle was first outlined by economist Fred Harrison, who identified that it has been occurring for hundreds of years[8] and it has since been expanded on and discussed by many scholars. The 18-year property cycle is used as a guideline by the world's most successful investors to make predictions on the market's next move.

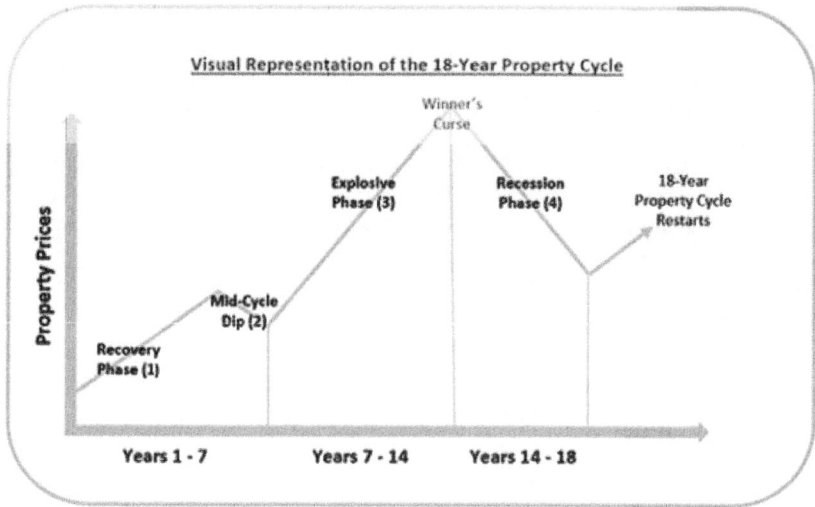

Visual Representation of the 18-Year Property Cycle

Winner's Curse

Explosive Phase (3)

Recession Phase (4)

18-Year Property Cycle Restarts

Mid-Cycle Dip (2)

Recovery Phase (1)

Property Prices

Years 1 - 7   Years 7 - 14   Years 14 - 18

With property investment, timing really is everything and by being aware of the 18-year property cycle, you can ensure that you are making the right decisions at the right time. It's particularly helpful to refer to when you are considering investments, choosing what kind of mortgages to apply for and when setting/re-evaluating your 1, 2 and 5-year strategies [3]. In order to build a successful portfolio, you must also buy, hold, and sell property depending on the phases of the cycle [23].

Let's consider the main characteristics of each of the four phases:

1. **Recovery Phase:** At the start of the recovery phase, property prices will be very low compared to the last few years as the market has just left a recession. These low prices, and the potential for high yields, will slowly encourage people to start buying property again. As the industry is still recovering from a recession, there won't be as many mortgages on offer whilst the market tries to recover, and people are still unsure if the recession is truly over.

71

2. **Mid-Cycle Dip:** At the end of the recovery phase there will be a short-lived dip. This is brought about by a temporary loss of confidence in the market, mixed in with a high-level of sales as investors and flippers release the capital gained during the recovery phase. The dip causes newspaper headlines to speculate that the market may be heading for a big downturn, and those who aren't aware of the 18-year property cycle will think this dip is the start of the next crash. Nonetheless, the professional property investor will remain confident knowing that phase 3 is just ahead.

3. **Explosive Phase:** A strong sign that things are on the up is when large corporations start to plan big developments. This gives the nation a bit more confidence that it's safe to start buying again, and both investors and homeowners will start purchasing. As more transactions occur within the industry property prices are pushed up.

By now, the property market is booming. The media is also reporting on the increase in sales which in turn fuels even more purchases. During this phase, lenders will be feeling generous, offering an array of deals to encourage people to buy.

As the market saturates, we reach what is called the '**Winner's Curse**'. This occurs right at the peak of the explosive phase. This is when prices are at their highest of the cycle, and phase 4 is right around the corner. The media will turn back to speculating about another crash.

4. **Recession Phase:** As confidence in the market starts to decline and the media goes on and on about impending doom, property demand starts to dwindle in what is almost a self-fulfilling prophecy. As demand declines, so do prices. Homeowners are much less

likely to move to a new house during this time, and investors hold out for the very end of the recession phase/start of the recovery phase to get good deals when they can be sure the property value won't drop below the purchase value. This is the phase that will distinguish the educated property developers from the novices.

The cycle is such an esteemed piece of work that it isn't hard to find out the current phase by doing a quick google search. However, if you take the time to research and identify the signs of the phases yourself, you will learn much more and come out on top.

The 18-year property cycle is covered further over the next two lessons [24 & 25].

24. IF YOU PURCHASE AT THE WRONG TIME, YOU RISK NEGATIVE EQUITY

Property investing is a *journey*. If you're in the property game for the long run, you will experience several rotations of the 18-year property cycle and therefore multiple ups and downs in the market. You must be ready for each phase and act appropriately during each. It's not about being active during booms and sitting out crashes.

Having learned the characteristics of each phase of the 18-year property cycle, we can determine when is a good or bad time to purchase property. This is important as if you buy at the wrong time the risk can be catastrophic, destroying your property portfolio completely.

Let's consider again the four phases of the 18-year property cycle, and what the best strategy in terms of holding, buying and selling would be in each case.

1. **Recovery Phase:** After a recession will always come recovery. Recovery indicates that the future of the property market is looking bright again. As prices begin to crawl back up, now is a great time to pur-

chase as you can be confident prices will increase further during the explosive phase. You will also benefit from properties being at the lowest market values of the new cycle. This means that your ROIs will be high, too. Only investors who desperately need to release capital or get rid of properties in negative equity will be selling during this time. Snap them up at bargain prices.

2. **Mid-Cycle Dip:** Don't let the temporary slip in the market fool you and be tempted to sell just yet. Hold onto your properties as they are about to increase significantly in value. However, you could take advantage of this little dip by easily obtaining a below market value deal.

3. **Explosive Phase:** From the start of the explosive phase, lenders will be feeling generous. This means you will be able to lock in some great mortgage rates. Your properties are set to increase in value over the next few years so hold off selling again. Any time within this phase will be a good time to buy - but the earlier you get in, the better.

Towards the end of the explosive phase, as prices reach their highest levels of the cycle and the next recession looms, now would not be such a good time to buy (you would be purchasing for a high price which is about to drop significantly in phase 4). This means that you could end up with a debt higher than the value of the property.

Instead, now would be an excellent time to recycle some of your property; selling your less lucrative investments at a high price, in order to release equity that you can reinvest in properties with better potential (higher yield, better THESIS © location or greater potential for capital growth) later on. If you do intend on selling property, this must be completed by the time the Winner's Curse ends.

4. **Recession Phase:** Hopefully your properties have been sufficiently stress-tested so that they can weather through phase 4, as now would be a terrible time to sell. Right at the start of the recession you shouldn't really be looking to buy, since prices are pretty much guaranteed to fall even further – although you might find some very good deals knocking around. Once you're well into the recession phase, and prices are at the lowest of the cycle, buying becomes a very viable opportunity. If you undertake any transactions during this time, be sure to put all potential investments through rigorous stress testing [40]. If you can make a profit now, these purchases will really flourish once the cycle restarts.

25. COVID (AND OTHER SIGNIFICANT EVENTS) CAN IMPACT THE 18-YEAR PROPERTY CYCLE

Although the 18-year property cycle is a fantastic market analysis tool, it should always be used as a guideline rather than a 100% guarantee.

Whilst the cycle will always move in the same order (recovery, mid-cycle dip, explosion, recession), the durations and severity of each phase will of course differ for each cycle. Furthermore, serious economic changes can threaten to 'reboot' the property cycle at any time. This occurred during both world wars and is at a risk of happening again as an effect of the pandemic. This means that the explosive phase could be more powerful than anticipated, or that the recession phase could be brought on earlier than expected... or exist for longer than usual.

As no one on this planet has ever experienced a global pandemic of this scale before, it is not possible to make strong predictions about how it will impact the property market and the 18-year property cycle. Yet we have already witnessed some consequences of it:

At the time of publishing this book, the pandemic had already led to a dramatic increase of properties being sold. This was initially due to many people seeking to upgrade their living arrangements after the UK experienced long periods of lockdown. As many people are now obliged to work from home and are going out much less, homes have taken on an even more important role than before.

According to several market analyses, property sales were at an all-time record high as of August 2020 and prices have increased nationwide by an average of 3% over Summer 2020[9]. Longer-lasting effects of COVID on the property cycle are yet to be seen, and it won't be until after they have occurred that we will be able to map out the effects on the 18-year property cycle chart.

My personal prediction is that the property market is currently either at the height of the explosive phase, or already within the Winner's Curse. Although property prices are currently high and the market is operating very strongly, (with estate agents reporting that they are absolutely inundated with work), I believe that this is not solely down to COVID causing a surge in people wanting to upgrade their homes. Personally, I believe that it is largely a combination of a backlog of transactions which weren't able to be carried out over the summer as the UK was in lockdown, and an influx of buyers who are speeding up a move/purchase due to the uncertainty of the future. Not only could we go back into lockdown at any time, but as furlough is set to end soon people who aren't confident that they will be able to apply for a mortgage in the near future (if they become unemployed) will be pushing forward with home moves now. Therefore, I believe that there are currently at least nine months of transactions being squeezed into a much shorter period.

If I had to put forward my own predictions for the future, I would guess that this 'boom' will be quite short lived, and we will experience a strong recession in the near future which must be heavily stress tested for. As with any recession, prices will drop significantly, and good deals could be made if investors have access to capital during this period.

I do believe that this is what many other investors are preparing for, as there are lots of relatively unexciting properties currently on the market listed 'with a tenant in place' which draws me to the conclusion that investors are getting rid of lower yielding properties in order to release equity ready to make new purchases during the recession.

I don't envisage the recession lasting longer than usual (around 4 years) but I do think that it will have stronger impacts than recent cycles. This is kind of obvious since we already know unemployment is soaring and many industries are struggling.

It would be totally arrogant and wrong of me to suggest you take my word for it. This is a very bold prediction and we will only know if I got it right in a few years' time. Many professional tycoons (who are significantly more successful than me) have other very different opinions on what the pandemic could mean for the 18-year property cycle and their opinions rarely align with each other. This further emphasises the uncertainty of the market and property cycle, and only time will tell who got it all right.

26. PROPERTIES TEND TO DOUBLE IN VALUE EVERY 9 YEARS

Over the last hundred years or so, property prices in the UK have increased on average by 100% every 9-10 years.

This is not to say that every single property in the UK doubles in value every nine years. Rather, the average value of the average property in the UK has doubled on average every nine years.

It is important to understand that this is a guideline and not a rule. Your property value is not guaranteed to double every nine years. It is highly dependent on the market and reliant on you carrying out research and buying property with potential. Even in booms, there will always be some properties that don't follow the norms and can even go down in value. For instance, consider a booming market but a terrible location with a worsening reputation. It isn't a pure fact and you can't come back in nine years and tell me off if your assets aren't all exactly twice as lucrative. We must also bear in mind the 18-year property cycle. One decade we could see a dramatic recession whereby prices fall, yet in the next decade we could experience a boom which would push property prices back to where they were and beyond.

Statistically speaking though, property prices on average

really have doubled in value approximately every nine years for over a century. This is due to things such as inflation [27] and demand. This is fantastic for making your money work for you.

These figures give us some confidence that our investments will increase in value over time. Despite pandemics, Brexit, inevitable market crashes, wars and everything in between, this statistic provides some reassurance that no matter what happens, our property investments will recover and even increase significantly in value overtime.

Don't just take my word for it; check out the market values doubling for yourself by visiting the land registry website where you will be able to view the UK House Price Index graphs on house prices over the years[10]. You can filter by property type, too, which is interesting as you will see variations across terraced, detached, semi-detached, and flats/maisonettes[11].

27. INFLATION MEANS INVESTING IN PROPERTY IS SAFER AND MORE LUCRATIVE THAN SAVING MONEY IN THE BANK

Inflation refers to the rise in general levels of prices of goods and services in the economy overtime.

In layman's terms, inflation is caused by supply and demand and from money being introduced into the economy.

As an illustrative example, imagine you bought a pint of milk 15 years ago for 20p. Today you couldn't buy the same pint of milk for 20p, because inflation has pushed up the cost to £1.20. Now imagine that you saved that 20p in the bank. Although you might have earned a little interest, you wouldn't be able to afford this pint of milk today with that money. Equally, if you had used your 20p to invest in the milk, your investment would be worth 6 times more, and you could sell it for a profit (OK the milk would be revolting but you get the point!).

As a result of this, if the capital you have in the bank is not earning the same level of interest as inflation, it will depreciate. Given that the bank also wants to make money, it is extremely unlikely that you will find a savings account earning the same or more than the inflation rate. This means that the interest you earn will always be lower than inflation. For example, if you receive 2% interest on money you save in the bank, and during this period inflation goes up by 3%, this means in the context of value appreciation you are actually losing money. To ensure that the value of your capital goes up with inflation, you would need to find a way to increase it by the same rate. This is why holding your cash in the bank can be a terrible idea. If you have ever wondered why people say £1,000,000 was worth more 5 years ago – this is why.

In contrast, property investing is an 'inflation beating asset'. This is because the value of property (and rental rates) increase in value in line with inflation.

28. THE HOUSING CRISIS IS A DOUBLE-EDGED SWORD.

The 'housing crisis' refers to a shortage in the number of homes being built compared with the number of homes required to meet demand. This supply and demand situation is another element that is pushing up the value of property.

Between 2006 and 2016 the UK population increased by 8% - the fastest ten-year growth in a century. This is largely due to migration and is expected to rise to nearly 70 million people by 2028, further fuelling the housing demand[12].

The need for more houses is also going up due to the increasing average life expectancy. In addition, there are now more people who live alone in single adult and single parent households, which increases the number of homes required per family. Changing trends on where people want to live means that there is a huge need for development in city centres, as this is the area where the fewest houses currently exist.

Due to these combined factors increasing the need for more homes, it is expected that there is currently a 'housing gap' of approximately 1.2 million homes in the UK[13].

Whilst the government has plans to tackle the housing crisis and bridge the housing gap, there are many hurdles in place. Firstly, there is a shortage of skilled labour to build the properties as quickly as is required. Furthermore, green belts are causing restrictions for building in popular areas where people want to live. For instance, there are many green belt areas around London and many northern cities including Manchester, Leeds and Birmingham where demand is high. Although governments have tried building on some green belts, there have been many protests from members of the public to protect these areas.

What is the government doing?

The government prioritises building new houses by setting themselves targets and preparing budgets. This includes many first-time buyer incentives to help people get on the property ladder.

But something doesn't quite line up. What would you build if there was a shortage of houses and in particular, affordable houses? Surely, moderately sized homes (probably terraced properties to get more houses in smaller spaces) would be a simple solution, right? Yet for some reason (ahem – profits!) these new build companies seem to be prioritising detached and semi-detached properties with additional downstairs toilets, en-suites and garages. Of course, the companies building these properties are still working in their own best interests, whilst demand is high profits are good. The companies are also competing with each other and supplying the UK with homes seems to be lower on the scale of priorities.

So, what does this mean for property investors?

The housing crisis is a double-edged sword for investors, as the existence of such lack of supply compared with a high demand is helpful for pushing up the value of property and yields greater returns whilst providing a large pool of potential tenants as the housing crisis fails to accommodate everyone. Looking ahead, rental properties should thrive for a long time as the proposals outlined to alleviate the housing crisis won't do enough since the factors contributing to it (migration, life expectancy, etc.) are estimated to continue rising at a much faster rate than new houses can be built.

Yet it's not something we investors can really rejoice in. Due to the housing crisis, the young adults of today are far less likely to be able to own their own home than previous generations due to the rising cost of property. Moreover, according to a report published by the BBC in 2020, a shortage of homes has contributed to poor living conditions for millions within the UK (homelessness, long council waiting lists, and people not being able to afford their own homes). As property investors, we need to step up and ensure that we are providing nice, safe and stable rented accommodation. Property investment is not only about profits - its personal. Renting is a solution for around 4.5 million households in the UK[14] and we should aspire to provide good homes for those who trust in us to do so.

PHASE TWO: CHOOSING INVESTMENTS

CHAPTER 5: RESEARCH

29. INVESTING IS NEVER A GAMBLE IF YOU DO YOUR RESEARCH

You may hear people or news articles talking about the risks of property investment.

There will always be people who see property investment as a risk due to a lack of property education or fear of crashes. As we have already covered, if you know how to anticipate moves in the market and how to act depending on which stage of the property cycle you are in, there are always smart choices that can make you a lot of money. It is actually thanks to the property cycle that the market is so lucrative.

Rest assured that property investments made using strong research strategies are always safe investments and very low in risk. Especially when compared to other investment strategies.

Many people think that their money is safer in a bank. Banks have been around a long time and pump a lot of capital into marketing their products as 'safe and reliable'. This is a generational mindset and due to inflation, we know that leaving large sums of money in the bank instead of investing it would be a terrible financial decision to make [27]. It also doesn't take a lot of googling to discover that over recent decades banks haven't been that 'safe and reliable' at all[15]!

Be sure to always keep your confidence no matter what the news might say or where we are in the cycle. If you make level-headed, well-researched decisions, you will always come out on top with property investment.

Research checklist to reduce risk:

- ✓ Location: THESIS ©
- ✓ Market: 18-year property cycle
- ✓ Finance: ROI, Gross Yield and Net Yield calculations
- ✓ Finding the right tenants
- ✓ Sourcing the right professionals and tradespeople
- ✓ Working towards end goals and constantly re-evaluating strategies

30. GET THE MOST OUT OF PROPERTY PORTALS

Most people only use online real-estate portals such as Rightmove and Zoopla to view properties that are currently on the market. Yet these property websites can offer so much more, especially to property investors.

Here are eight ways that you can use property portals to their full potential to gain priceless benefits:

1. **Area stats**: Search by postcode to view market trends broken down and represented on graphs. These give you great visual guides on how the market has been doing in that area and an indication of the potential an area has. From here, you can also follow links to the next benefit; the listing history.

2. **View listing history**: Using property portals will also give you access to land registry information on the selling prices of properties filtered to your chosen focus. If these properties were previously listed on the portal, you will also be able to view the original listing on the site (including photos) which will give you a great indication of the condition of the property when it was sold at that price.

3. **Research estate agents**: By searching by agent, you can view all properties listed by specific agencies. This is helpful when you are considering which

agency to use to list or manage your property. By comparing their property descriptions and quality of photographs, you can get great insight into how your property would be marketed by each agency. This will help you choose which one is the best since it isn't just the fees that are important to decision making. Furthermore, if you're looking to let in a new area, you can search rental properties by location to quickly see which agencies are operating there.

4. **Know how to present your property**: When you are preparing your property to go to market, research similar properties in the area that have recently sold/been tenanted to see how they were decorated and what was included/not included. Don't consider those still on the market as they haven't yet successfully attracted anyone so might not be good examples. Make notes on what you like about each property, and then apply these findings to your own to give you the best appeal.

5. **Search based on time to travel to major locations**: This is a great tool for researching potential ripple effect [37] areas. Rather than searching for properties within certain locations, both Zoopla and Rightmove have great functions that allow you to search and filter property that is accessible in a given travel time (filtered to your chosen travel method). This will help you to discover new, easily commutable areas, compare prices across similarly distanced towns, and find ripple effect locations that will increase in appeal once the hotspot [36] becomes saturated.

6. **Draw your own search areas**: Using the 'draw-a-search' tool, you can set up your own custom maps by drawing around the areas that you are interested in. For instance, drawing around a main road leading out of a city centre that covers two different towns. You might not be interested in the towns per se, or

the streets more than a couple of minutes' walk from the road/local shops/train station, etc. So, a simple search of those towns would not be useful. Once you draw your own search area, you can set up notifications so that you are alerted as soon as a property within that search becomes available or is reduced. Use the various filters (price, property type, number of bedrooms...) to focus your alerts on exactly what you're looking for.

7. **Enhance your buyer power using property trackers**: These are plug-ins which enable you to see the history of property transactions overtime. For instance, this could include alterations that have been made to listings. You also will be able to see properties which are under offer and any history of offers falling through. By having this insider information, you will be able to prepare a better approach to your own offer. For instance, if you find out that a seller recently accepted a below market value offer which fell through, you could make that same offer whilst emphasising your reliability and readiness to complete a purchase. Recommended plug-ins include Property Tracker, Nethouseprices and Property-bee.

8. **Access to published reports**: Rightmove publishes a highly valuable market trends report and price comparison report. Equally, Zoopla offers some useful 'Zooplomas' – (property guides) and UK area stats including property value data and graphs.

31. THINK WITH YOUR HEAD NOT YOUR HEART - BUT TRUST YOUR GUT

When investing in property, it is really important to think with your head and not your heart. In an exciting industry like property investment, it's easy for some people to forget the numbers and 'fall in love' with a property or location without thinking it through completely.

When deciding on a property to invest in, it is essential that you make your decision by running the numbers [38] and making logical conclusions. Don't invest in a property that you love because of its beautiful garden and location if the net yield would be poor.

Whilst first impressions can be very important, don't get carried away by external factors such as pressure from an agency to make a quick decision. Make sure that your head is working hard to determine the real value of the property and create limitations for yourself which will impede you from making any reckless decisions.

Your personalised limitations should be created in line with any weaknesses that you identify within your own decision-making process, and you should enforce them very strictly, not allowing for any exceptions. Whist it may occasionally feel that your own rules are causing you to miss out on a deal, remember that if a property doesn't meet your full criteria, it can't be the deal of a lifetime.

Setting yourself strict rules to follow will enable you to trust that your decision-making process is safe and should stop you from getting carried away on a deal that might not be as great as it first appeared.

Here is an example of three limitations you could adopt:

1. I will not buy ANY property that has a yield lower than X%, no matter what.
2. I will only purchase property that is at least X% below what I determine to be the market value.
3. I will not put in an offer on ANY property without considering it for at least X hours.

The exception to listening to your head and not your heart, is to trust your gut. Have you ever encountered a good deal on paper, yet you still felt unsure or uneasy about it? That's your gut talking to you. Let's say for example that you run the numbers on a three-bed in Newcastle and everything looks great; except that your gut has a bad feeling about it. Perhaps you get the impression that it may be difficult to get good tenants in this area, or that you feel the seller isn't telling you absolutely everything. If your gut is trying to tell you something, listen to it. Do not back out of a deal just because your gut instinct is not speaking the same language as the numbers you run, but use that gut feeling to dig deeper.

32. IF YOU FEEL RUSHED, IT'S PROBABLY NOT A GOOD DEAL

The best property investment deals and opportunities will be the ones that you find yourself, by using the research methods provided in this book and by taking the time to make well-educated decisions.

What you must be aware of, is that during your property journey you will find that there are also many people whose job it is to encourage you to make certain purchases.

Professionals such as new build sales representatives, estate agents and property advice specialists like brokers and sourcers, all work on commission and target-based incentives. To them you are a potential buyer and just as in any retail store they will try to encourage you to make particular purchases in order to reach their own targets and earn a living. Their persuasion and sales techniques won't always be in your best interest, but it certainly will be in theirs.

Whilst by no means is this lesson aimed at demeaning the professions of these individuals, it is important to learn that despite the encouragement from external contributors, you must ensure you make the right decision by listening only to your own best judgement, researching your locations, asking the right questions and calculating and stress testing the numbers

[40]. It is of course the case that many deals can be mutually beneficial to both parties, such as an estate agent showing you a great property that has a good ROI and which they will also gain commission from selling.

Know how to recognise sales techniques so that you don't fall into the trap of believing a property has more potential than it possibly has. If a professional tells you that a particular property can attain a certain yield, dig deep to find out how that figure was reached.

The most common technique used within the property market is promoting a sense of urgency to the sale. For instance, letting you know that there is a lot of interest in a particular property or informing you there is a limited time left on a deal.

Yes, you may need to act fast when you come across a great opportunity in order to seal the deal before another investor makes a better offer to the seller, but the only person who should be pushing you... is you. You should always have everything in place to allow you to move as quickly as you need to, without feeling rushed.

Another technique is that you will be contacted regarding an 'opportunity' that you hadn't sought out yourself. This can be the case when companies who sell property gain access to your contact details. If you receive a call offering you a great deal, or get an email about a new development, ignore it!

People shouldn't need to be persuaded to take a great deal, so if you feel as though you are being pushed to say yes or have identified some typical sales strategies, consider this a red flag.

As a general rule, good deals do not land on your lap - you have to go out and work hard to find and negotiate them. If it's too sales-led, or if the deals find you... avoid at all costs!

33. LOOK FOR PROPERTIES WHERE VALUE CAN BE ADDED THRICE

During your research stage of property investment, you should be looking out for the potential to add value to property thrice. Before making an offer on any property, always ask yourself this simple question: Can I add value to this property thrice?

In order to buy smart, purchase property that has the potential to have value added to it in three different ways. The first two add value at the purchase stage and require no additional capital investment to do so. The final value-adding strategy involves investing an amount of money into the property in order to improve it to a level whereby the overall value of the property will increase by a significantly larger amount than the capital used.

Value 1: Location

The first way that you should always add value to a property is by buying in the right location. Using THESIS © [35] to identify ripple effects [37], you should be able to find locations which have the potential to go up in value higher than inflation in the short and long-term future. Make it a priority to invest in areas that are not only going to appeal to tenants or buyers in the short term, but that are highly likely to become even more desirable overtime. As demand for that location grows, so will your market value. Being able to differentiate between a property that is in a great location and a property that is in a location that will become great will result in your property's value growing much quicker.

Value 2: Buy Below Market Value (BMV)

Secondly, add value to your property by purchasing BMV. The benefits of buying BMV include taking on less debt and being able to use leverage in the future [57]. By purchasing BMV, you could potentially refinance the property to gain access to funds[16], or sell the property for a profit after capital gains tax [64].

Value 3: Refurbish

Finally, buy property that has the potential to be improved in one way or another. This could be as simple as refreshing the décor of the property from outdated wallpaper and flooring to a more neutral interior, or even go as far as to add an extension or en-suite to the property. Adding value through renovation and improvements, also referred to as forced equity, will increase the property's value which will in turn allow you to either sell for a profit later along the line or release equity through a remortgage to help finance the next venture.

CHAPTER 6: LOCATION

34. A PROPERTY'S VALUE IS LARGELY BASED ON LOCATION

When it comes to property investment, it is not only what's on the inside that counts. You could buy the most beautiful house with spacious bedrooms, huge gardens, a top-notch kitchen and a converted loft – but if it's in a terrible area, no one will want to rent or buy it.

This is because the value of a property is largely determined by the area it is in, and what similar houses have sold for recently.

When your property is valued, the surveyor will already have a pretty good idea of how much they will value your property at, based on the location and how much other properties have sold in that area in the past. They will approach the property with a roundabout figure already in mind and then check out the condition of the inside, structure and outdoor areas, to decide if your property is at the higher or lower end of that figure.

A quick online search of similar properties in the area will give you a good indication of the price, and you can view photographs of the properties to understand what gives some a higher valuation over others.

Remember that streets and broader locations will always have a valuation 'cap'. This means that no matter how furnished on the inside a property may be, the properties in that area won't go beyond a certain price bracket. For instance, the most luxurious property, with gold taps and crystal floors will not sell for millions if it is located in a run-down area where the average property price is £90,000. However, if you could pick up that property and drop it in the centre of London, it would increase in value significantly.

35. LOOK FOR THESIS ©

The most effective way to research potential areas for investment is to apply the THESIS © analysis. This research method covers everything that must be considered when seeking lucrative locations to invest in. Using THESIS © will not only help you identify areas which are most likely to see house price values increase in the short to medium term, but it is also a highly effective tool for identifying areas suitable for your target markets.

THESIS © stands for <u>Transport</u>, <u>Health Care</u>, <u>Employment</u>, <u>Schools</u>, <u>Investment</u> and <u>Shops</u>. These six categories make up the formula for the perfect location. Locations that stand up well against these six categories will have the better potential for capital growth and good yields.

It's important to consider the potential of an area as well as the its current state. If you are looking for ripple effect towns near to a hotspot, locations that already have THESIS © will be good contenders. If you are looking for strong capital growth overtime, you should be more interested in finding locations where THESIS © will be significantly improved in the future.

Whilst it is fantastic if you can identify an area which ticks all six of the THESIS © boxes, a great location can be one which ticks only some of them, (relevant to you target market[17]) and has future development plans to attain or improve on the rest. For instance, a studio flat in a city centre might not need to be located near to a good school if you are targeting businesspeople. Equally, a cosy bungalow targeting retired people may not be affected by a location's plans to improve the transport links into a major city centre, but it might add to the capital growth of the area overtime.

Use the tools available on property websites such as Rightmove and Zoopla to conduct your THESIS © research, as well as local council websites and simple google searches. It can also be quick and easy to spend time driving around an area or visiting it virtually via google maps to continue your research and learn more about the surrounding areas. Finally, networking with other investors or people who live in your area of interest can prove highly effective, too.

To carry out your THESIS © research, please refer to the THESIS © outline in the bonus material section at the end of this book, which will provide you with a comprehensive list of THESIS © considerations.

Present your THESIS © analysis in the form of a professional report. Even if the location you research doesn't fit what you're looking for right now, you never know when you might pick up the analysis again and reconsider the area for a future investment. If your analysis is successful and you decide to invest in that area, you could even provide an (edited) copy of it to potential buyers/tenants as marketing material to promote the area and increase interest on your property.

Consider compiling a **SWOT** (**S**trengths, **W**eaknesses, **O**pportunities, **T**hreats) analysis of each of the six THESIS © categories. A SWOT analysis pushes you to consider every pro and con of the area in question so that you have a well-rounded, unbiased analysis.

The THESIS © analysis is one of the most important phases of your property research. Every investment must start with the selection of an area. When it comes to investing, you are not only investing in bricks and mortar, but land, too and the area is 99% of what your tenants/buyers will be interested in. You must always choose your area first and your property second. Once you have selected your area of choice, choosing a property is easy.

36. AVOID HOTSPOTS

Locations labelled as hotspots are areas which have been identified as popular places in which to purchase property at a particular time. A hotspot is an unofficial term and is usually chosen by the media or investment marketing companies, based on past purchase history and existing demand.

A lot of investors can be tempted to plan their next purchase in hotspot areas, but it's only really useful to know where hotspots are, in order to identify what locations were lucrative to purchase in the past, as once they hit hotspot status it's no longer the best area to invest in.

Information on hotspots is usually released in response to a demand by (slightly lazy) investors to learn where they should make investments without having to do any of their own research. This cutting corner technique can be detrimental since once a list of hotspots reaches the public, there is often a surge in demand for this area which pushes up prices even further, thus reducing the potential for good investments.

The best way to benefit from hotspots is to identify them before anyone else does. This is done by carrying out research on several locations to identify which areas have the most potential to increase in value based on development plans and buying patterns.

Once a location is publicly identified as a hotspot, it will likely be too late to grab a great deal there. However, there is one way that you can benefit from hotspots, and that is to use them to identify ripple effects [37] and invest in those areas instead.

37. LOOK OUT FOR THE RIPPLE EFFECT

In property terms, the ripple effect refers to the wave of property prices and demand increasing outwards from a central area of high activity. Ripple effects are usually caused by popular areas becoming so expensive or saturated that new buyers are forced to consider locations just outside of that area. Just like throwing a pebble into a river, the ripple effect doesn't stop there, and more and more ripples are created as the neighbouring areas become more popular and people are forced even further away from the initial area of interest.

A really easy visual representation of the ripple effect can be seen by looking at a map of the London Tube zones (this also works quite literally too). As the very centre of London (Zone 1) became completely saturated and extremely expensive to purchase in, buyers sought the closest next best thing (Zone 2). Once Zone 2 became saturated, prices in that area also rose and people started to look for the second next best thing (Zone 3) and so on.

Understanding the ripple effect is just the first step. Once we understand it, we can learn to anticipate it, and this is a key tool to finding great locations that are likely to increase in value. It's incredibly easy to identify which large towns and cities are most desirable – just look around! You will find popular businesses moving into the area, or new investments in the local infrastructure. You can also visit government websites to identify key development areas. Those areas which are already considered hotspots will be the ones which cause ripple effects since they are already expensive and in huge demand.

Using hotspots as your central point, research nearby towns. Find out which towns tick the THESIS © boxes, in particular offering quick access to the hotspot area (e.g. a short train ride or well-connected roads). Then consider any development plans in the pipelines. Remember that you won't be the very first person to 'discover' the ripple effect. Large businesses will already have done plenty of research into ripple effect areas and their plans are tell-tale signs of where the next sought out place could be. Look out for new build property plans to construct in nearby towns, any plans to open new supermarkets or upmarket shops (Waitrose is a great one to watch out for) and government plans to plough money into 'regeneration areas'. Follow the money, but make sure that you get in there as early as possible, before the hype begins.

CHAPTER 7: NUMBER CRUNCHING

38. UNDERSTAND YIELD

Yield can initially sound a bit tricky but it's actually very simple to understand and calculate. There are two different yield calculations: gross yield and net yield. The only difference between the two is that gross yield considers the rental income and net yield considers the rental profit.

Yields tell you the percentage of return per annum that you would gain from the property, compared to its initial cost.

For both net and gross yields, the higher the percentage, the more favourable an investment (from a numerical analysis only).

Gross Yield – Good for comparing opportunities quickly

Gross yield is a good calculation for investors looking to quickly allocate a figure to a property in order to compare it against others. The percentage will appear higher than net yield as it doesn't take into consideration any costs associated with owning and renting the property.

For this reason, gross yield is only really useful when compared with other properties to see which come out on top and which potential investments are less financially attractive. Gross yield isn't fully reliable, as it doesn't consider costs. This means that whilst a high rental income could mean the gross yield percentage seems high, if the costs of owning and running the property are very expensive, it might not be a good investment at all.

Be aware of anyone trying to sell you a property by quoting

a good gross yield instead of net yield, as it doesn't give the full picture or tell you how much profit you would make after costs are considered. If a seller is focussed on the gross yields, it could be a red flag for high costs.

$$\text{Gross Yield} = \frac{\text{Annual Rental Income}}{\text{Purchase Price}} \times 100$$

Example:

2-bed mid-terraced property in Liverpool	
Purchase Price	£100,000
Deposit (25%)	£25,000
Expected Annual Rental Income	£9000

Gross Yield: (£9000 ÷ £100,000) X 100 = 9%.

Working out this gross yield allows you to quickly compare different properties against each other, to see which come out on top.

Net Yield – More realistic insight to a property's value to an investor – requires a slightly trickier calculation

The most common of the two yield calculations is net yield. This is because it is a lot more reliable as a profit indicator since it takes into consideration all costs that owning and renting the property will incur. Investors use net yield to consider potential investments and to re-evaluate how successful their existing properties are. If a property is becoming less beneficial due to rising running costs, a net yield calculation will identify this, and a solution can be sought.

For net yield, the annual rental profit is calculated by deducting all costs associated with running the property from the annual rental income. Costs include, but are not limited to, mortgage payments, insurance payments and estate agent fees. The more costs you anticipate, the safer your calculation will be. If you can consider multiple potential costs (for instance including repairs and anticipated void periods) and still obtain good results, you can be more confident that your property will be lucrative in times of hardship, and even more lucrative in favourable climates.

$$\text{Net Yield} = \frac{\text{Annual Rental Profit}}{\text{Purchase Price}} \times 100$$

Example:

2-bed mid-terraced property in Liverpool	
Purchase Price	£100,000
Deposit (25%)	£25,000
Expected Annual Rental Income	£9000
(Rental Cost) Agency fee of 10%	-£900
(Rental Cost) Void Allowance (1 month)	-£750
(Rental Cost) Insurances	-£200
(Rental Cost) Mortgage Repayments [3% Interest Only]	-£2250
Total Rental Costs	-£4100
Rental Profit	£4900

Net Yield: (£4900 ÷ £100,000) X 100 = 4.9%.

Now we have a realistic figure, we can compare this against the net yields of other potential investments to see which is the most lucrative.

39. ALWAYS CALCULATE RETURN ON INVESTMENT (ROI)

ROI is the most useful calculation out of the three, as it considers your actual capital input into the property and ignores the good debt (mortgage) held on it. ROI tells us how much of the capital invested we will get back each year (and therefore, how long it will take us to make our money back before we are running at a pure profit).

Similar to net yield, include as many costs as you can to work out the profit. Capital used to purchase includes all costs (big and small) required to buy the property. This can include the deposit, solicitor fees, broker fees, surveyor fees, refurbishment costs, etc.). It does not include any mortgage taken out on the property.

$$ROI = \frac{\text{Annual Rental Profit}}{\text{Capital Used to Purchase}} \times 100$$

Example:

2-bed mid-terraced property in Liverpool	
Purchase Price	£100,000
Deposit (25%)	£25,000
Legal fees, professional fees and stamp duty	£6000
Expected Annual Rental Income	£9000
(Rental Cost) Agency fee of 10%	-£900
(Rental Cost) Void Allowance (1 month)	-£750
(Rental Cost) Insurances	-£200
(Rental Cost) Mortgage Repayments [3% Interest Only]	-£2250
Total Rental Costs	-£4100
Rental Profit	£4900

ROI: (£4900 ÷ £31000) X 100 = 15.8%.

If I get 15.8% of my capital invested back each year, it will take me roughly 6.4 years to regain the capital invested.

This result is quite a decent ROI which indicates that this could be a good potential investment. But it's still important to check that the yields are also strong and if it might be possible to obtain even better numbers from other opportunities, as well as seeing what the qualitative research indicates.

To take these calculations further, I could play around with the costs to see how my yields and ROI would look like under different scenarios (e.g. higher interest rates). This is called stress testing.

40. STRESS TEST

When running numbers for your key calculations, it is very important to run realistic predictions, rather than running numbers optimistically.

When considering costs, always allow for things to go wrong. This is not to say you should expect the worst, but you should accept that things will not always go exactly to plan. Refurbishments can often bring up unexpected additional jobs that must be carried out, solicitors can sometimes uncover certain things that need to be addressed, and deadlines are often overrun which can also increase void periods.

Let's say you are thinking about buying a property and the numbers look great. The property ticks all the THESIS © boxes and based on current interest rates your net profit will be very healthy. But what if interest rates go up after one or two years? Would you still make a decent profit? At what point would you start making a loss? If we move into a recession phase, where would you stand?

If you were to run your numbers optimistically selecting figures that you are hopeful to achieve rather than guaranteed to achieve, you leave no margin of error to cover yourself in a worst-case scenario. The investment therefore appears more lucrative. This can only cause complications in the long run and is extremely dangerous.

By stress testing your properties you can be certain that, should something unexpected occur whilst you own the property, your finances will still hold strong without running into negative equity. Stress testing is also essential to demonstrate the ROI and net yield you can expect when the market becomes less favourable. Investors should be looking to invest for the long-term, which means that the property will need to be held throughout periods of recession. To that end, you need to be certain that any property you invest in will be able to yield good returns for you even when the market is less favourable.

The Property Life ROI, Yield and Stress Test Calculator © allows you to easily stress test any of your current or potential investments. You can access this by visiting www.property-life.co.uk/resources.

How to stress test:

1. Using the spreadsheet, run your numbers realistically, whilst erring on the side of caution. In the Property Life spreadsheet, the formula for determining ROI and yields are already inputted so you just need to add in the property specific numbers.
2. Next, adjust the figures in the stress test column to reflect any possible additional costs. The results will show you if you would still be OK if unexpected issues were to arise. If the results show that it would be tough to recover from any of the above, then perhaps it's not worth taking the risk in this instance. If the results show that the property would still run at a profit and be able to weather through a recession or unexpected issue, you can be more confident in the success of the property.
3. Finally, stress test the figures even further by editing the figures reliant on the market. Change the interest rates several times to see how much 'stress' this investment could handle before it runs into negative equity.

Once you have run these numbers, it will be much easier to make educated decisions on which properties you are prepared to invest your money in. If your potential new property can survive stress testing, you can purchase confidently and keep your cool when everyone else is getting hot under the collar during the tougher phases, knowing that you'll make it out the other side OK.

Equally, if you discover that the property you are looking into wouldn't produce great financial results, this doesn't mean you have to walk away from the investment. Instead you can use this information to help you negotiate a better purchase price that would mean your properties can survive the stress testing. You can stress test the purchase price on the spreadsheet to find out at what point the property would be a lucrative purchase to help you decide what below market value offer to make.

CHAPTER 8: TYPES OF INVESTMENT

41. LET TO YOUR LOCAL COUNCIL

Many local councils across the UK rent properties from investors and sublet them to their own tenants. There are pros and cons to subletting, as outlined below.

Pros:

- The council rent according to a guaranteed rent scheme, which means you will receive rent whether someone is in the property or not.
- Although the council offer between 20-30% less rent than if you were to rent privately, this is outweighed by the fact that you don't need to pay an agency to manage the property and won't experience any void periods.
- The council also takes care of any certificate renewals that are required, including paying the associated fees.
- In some cases - if the council has a budget allocated at the time of acquisition - they might refurbish your property free of charge, in order to raise it to their own standards. This in turn is likely to increase the value of your property without you spending a penny or requiring any of your time.
- Contracts tend to be 5-10 years, giving you a guaranteed rental income for a long period.
- Since the council take care of everything, you can enjoy a completely hands-off approach and focus your energy on other investments.

Cons:

- As with any contract, should you exit early, you will be liable to early exit fees which will be outlined in your contract.
- You won't have control over who the council sublets the property to, and it's likely that they will be Local Housing Allowance (LHA) tenants who are typically less desirable to private landlords.
- Before you can let to the council, you must obtain a mortgage and building insurance that allows subletting, or request permission from your current providers to change the conditions of your contract. As there are less products on offer for properties let to the council, rates on mortgages and insurance are usually less favourable than for a standard buy-to-let property.
- The rent you receive from the council remains the same for the duration of your contract and does not increase each year in line with inflation.

To find out if this is a viable option for you, simply contact local councils to enquire if they are seeking properties and if so, what type they currently require (family homes, bungalows, 3-beds, etc.).

Consider the pros and cons carefully before deciding if this strategy could be for you. Generally, if you find a council that are looking for properties to sublet and have budgets allocated for refurbishments, it can be a great first project for new investors as you will learn a lot about the renting process whilst being significantly hands off and low-risk. Remember that you won't receive your first payment until any essential work has been completed and their tenant enters the property - so make sure you can cover the cost of the property until then.

42. RENT-TO-RENT IS A GREAT WAY TO GET EXPERIENCE WITH LOWER RISK

Rent-to-rent is the process whereby you rent a property from an owner, with the intention of subletting it out to your own tenants. It's a great strategy for those looking to make money through renting property and get experience as a landlord without the need for a large upfront sum.

Generally, rent-to-rent works by renting a property for a higher cost than what you are paying the owner. The difference (minus your costs) being your profit. It is not uncommon to see this strategy used for HMO rentals. The investor pays the landlord a standard rental fee each month, but they sublet it to multiple paying tenants, allowing for a larger profit.

It's not as straightforward as it might seem, however. First of all, the owner of the property would need permission from their lender and insurer to allow the property to be sublet, which can be a lengthy process. Secondly, there would be many regulations that you must also adhere to, such as getting permission to run an HMO and you may also need to inform the local council of the agreement. For this reason, it can be tricky to find a suitable property with an owner who is willing to jump through any required hoops to ultimately benefit you.

One way to appeal to property owners, is to guarantee rent.

This means that the owner would receive an income each month, regardless of if the property was tenanted or not. To offset the risk of this, a slightly below average rent can be agreed that allows you to save for any void periods. As you would be assuming the role of the landlord, as well as being the owner's tenant, the owner would be considerably hands free which would benefit them further. The benefits must add up for the owner. Otherwise, if they would be better off letting the property under a standard tenancy agreement, you won't get a look in.

But there are of course drawbacks, and the largest of all is the fact that rent-to-rent does not involve any ownership of the property. This means that you can't benefit from inflation or leverage. Additionally, as you don't own the property this can't be considered as an investment[18] – but it is excellent education and experience. It also involves putting a lot of trust into the owner, to maintain their side of the contract (keeping up with mortgage payments, for instance). As a rule, rent-to-rent is a good strategy for those just starting out or who may not have enough to pay a deposit on a buy-to-let mortgage but want to build capital and save for future investments whilst gaining property experience.

43. FLATS HAVE GREAT CAPITAL GROWTH - BUT MORE RISK

According to a recent survey, 87% of investors prefer to invest in houses rather than flats[19]. This is despite the fact that flats typically have much better capital growth.

When it comes to investing in property, it's natural to find that you have a preference when it comes to purchasing either houses or flats. This could be because of a gut instinct, previous experience or where you have lived in the past.

As a general rule, when you run the numbers, flats in city centres will usually offer you greater capital growth than houses.

Here are three reasons why:

1. It is said that flats grow in value faster than any other property type.
2. Flats require less personal maintenance than houses (no gardens, less rooms, etc.).
3. Flats tend to exist where demand for residential accommodation is required most and rent is higher than average[20].

However, there are also some downsides associated with flats. For instance:

1. With flats, you have no opportunity to extend or conduct large renovation works making it harder to significantly increase the value of the property once you own it, other than through inflation.
2. There is usually a higher turnover in tenants in flats than in houses - meaning more void periods.
3. Flats tend to be leasehold meaning you will have service charges to pay. The costs of these charges are out of your control so they could increase during your ownership, and the future of the building is never guaranteed. The companies who manage flats/landlords are also renown for being a little difficult to deal with.
4. As several residences are connected under one roof, other people can negatively affect the quality of the building and experience of the tenant/s (e.g. risk of fire, damage to communal areas and higher levels of noise as you can have neighbours above and below, not just to the sides).

Ultimately, it will come down to your personal preferences and what you feel most comfortable in dealing with. Just because flats yield higher returns on average does not mean that you should only aim to invest in flats, or that any flat is a better investment than any house. Choose each property carefully. The best and safest strategy is to always have a diversified property portfolio, so that if one type of property is affected, your entire portfolio won't suffer the same consequences.

44. CONSIDER BUNGALOWS

The most common rental properties are terraced houses (36%) and flats (37%). This is followed by semi-detached (16%) and detached houses (6%). Bungalows sit right at the end of the scale at just 4%[21]. It's therefore clear that bungalows are not an investor's first (or even second, third or fourth) choice when the time comes to purchase property. However, investors are really missing a trick. Bungalows offer great investment opportunities and should be considered much more. When you start to look for your next property, make sure to check out any available bungalows.

Here's why:

1. **The population is ageing.** With people living longer, there are more over 60s than ever before. This ageing population needs suitable places to live and there are simply not enough bungalows out there to meet demand. This means that many people who require or prefer bungalows due to their personal situations can find it very difficult to source one in their desired area. Consequently, due to supply and demand, the rental profits on bungalows can be very lucrative.

2. **The government forgot about bungalows.** The government is trying to build as many houses as it can to tackle the housing shortage in the UK, but they haven't really taken our ageing population into consideration. Most new build companies are focussed on multi-storey homes or flats. Existing bungalows

are quickly becoming a hot commodity.

3. **Over 60s make great tenants**. This target market has a very good reputation for treating property well, meaning there are minimal damages or refurbishment work required between tenants. Older tenants are (usually) easy to manage and are often looking to reside in a property long-term (often for the remaining years of their lives). Finally, they are reliable. Their rent will often come from pensions[22] or savings rather than be dependent on income from employment.

If you do get your hands on a bungalow, ensure that it is in an area where demand for this type of accommodation will be high and, if you are targeting the older generations, make sure that it is fully safe and easy to live in. The property should offer easy access, be wheelchair friendly, have accessible bathrooms (consider a walk-in shower, for instance) and be easily secured. When you welcome a tenant into the property, find out if there are any adaptations you could make to enhance their experience of living in their new home. If your tenant has any particular requirements or concerns, you could adjust the property accordingly. Remember a successful investor isn't only in it for the profits – you must conduct your business ethically and with respect, too.

45. THEY DON'T ALL HAVE TO BE HOMES.

When you mention buy-to-let, property investment or tenant-ing, most people will naturally think of residential property. However, it is also possible - and just as straightforward - to rent property to companies. Let's look at two different pur-chase options that include companies as the tenant.

1. **Mixed-Use:** This is a kind of 'half and half' strat-egy, whereby you own a property which is rented to both a residential tenant and a company. This com-monly takes the form of a ground floor shop with a flat above it. This is often the case with many high streets in small to medium-sized towns. Next time you drive through a main road full of shops, look up and you will most likely see signs of residential living above ground-floor businesses. Mixed-use properties are beneficial for small business owners who want to rent a shop space and residential space so that they can live where they work. But it can also be con-sidered as two totally separate entities, whereby you rent the commercial space to a company and find a tenant with no connection to the business for your residential space.

2. **Commercial:** This refers to property which has no residential terms connected to it. Commercial build-ings include all types of properties used for running any type of business (from hotels and pubs, to office buildings and betting shops). The property can be

rented wholly to one company for their sole use, or in parts to several different companies.

Renting to companies rather than individuals can be very advantageous as they tend to yield a higher return on investment compared to residential properties and successful companies tend to stay in one place longer than residential tenants. Another benefit is that many companies will fully decorate and furnish the spaces themselves. Franchises and chains in particular will have a very specific way of presenting a space (such as fast-food restaurant chains that appear identical to one another), meaning you often do not even need to provide flooring or painted walls.

As with any type of investment strategy, there are certain legislations in place for commercial property. Before purchasing a property with the intention to use it for commercial purposes, you must check that it is legally permitted for such use and would comply with any regulations surrounding commercial zoning, if relevant. You can easily do this by getting in touch with the local council that the property sits within.

One major consideration to make in the current market, is that it is clear that more and more commercial companies are relying on their online presence and removing themselves gradually from highstreets and local areas. This has made investing on local high-streets more high risk.

COVID has further contributed to a work-from-home culture with many office spaces becoming obsolete. Yet there will always be a need for certain commercial spaces. Companies providing physical services such as convenience stores, garages and hairdressers will always be around, making them good target markets for mixed-use or commercial investments. The key is to research the location in detail and identify opportunities. There is no use investing in a space hoping to appeal to hairdressers if there are already five established hairdressers within a 1-mile radius.

46. A HOUSE IS NOT A HOME IS NOT A HOUSE

Know the difference between a house and a home because, generally speaking, one is an asset and the other is a liability [8].

A house is a property which you can purchase as a tangible asset that can generate cash for you. A home is a place that you live in and which costs money to do so. It does not generate money. A house is professional. A home is personal.

A property can be considered a house to one person (such as an investor) and a home to another person (such as a tenant). For the tenant, it is considered a liability, whilst for the investor it is a debt beating, leverage holding, inflation beating asset that can appreciate THRICE [33].

Everyone – even the savviest property investor - will live in a home, regardless of if they own it or it is owned by someone else. A home is essential, keeps us warm, dry and safe and is usually decorated to our own personal tastes and requirements.

Being able to comprehend the differences between a house and a home should help you get a good grasp on the following two important take-aways:

1. **Professionally:** Remember that the houses we own are homes for others. A good property investor should not only focus on the profits but be conscious

of the fact that they are providing a home to someone that requires it. Investors should have a sense of responsibility and duty of care to their tenants. They should ensure the house provides a safe and welcoming home for those who are putting money in your pockets. It is the considerate investor who will have the most success because they fully comprehend the market and carry out their responsibilities effectively.

2. **Personally**: Whilst your own home will still be considered a liability in technical terms. Take action to make your home as much of an asset as possible. Although it will cost you money to live in your home, you can still aim to add value to your property, meaning the property you own will be worth more than the debt you owe. Also, recognise the monetary value in owning your own home rather than renting. It is almost always cheaper to pay a mortgage than it is to pay rent (which is essentially paying someone else's mortgage plus a profit). Despite this, it is true that some property investors do prefer to rent. It is good insider research and is suitable for those who don't want to be tied down to one particular location.

47. A GOOD HMO COULD GET YOU FINANCIALLY FREE IN ONE GO

According to the Gov.uk website, a House in Multiple Occupation (HMO) is a property rented out by at least three people who are not from one 'household' but share facilities like the bathroom and kitchen. It is sometimes called a 'house-share'[23].

HMOs can sometimes bring in enough revenue to get you financially free in one go. This of course would be an exceptional HMO and depend on your financially free number. But far from a sweeping statement, if you really put in the time to research the right property and obtain it below market value with a good interest-only mortgage, tenanting it as an HMO could yield excellent returns.

If this seems rather elaborate for your plans, consider the possibility that renting a three-bed property to three individuals rather than to a small family could significantly enhance your rental income. This is based on the average that a three-bed property in the North-East rents at £850.00 whilst a three-bed property share could easily rent at £450 per bedroom. This is a total of £1,350 - £500 more income each month.

Of course, HMOs come with a lot of responsibility as more tenants equals more maintenance, admin and risk, plus a typically higher turnover rate with more frequent void periods. One of the most important things with an HMO is to choose your tenants very carefully. All tenants under one roof should be within the same target market to help ease the co-habiting process.

HMOs should be at least partly furnished, if not fully furnished, as tenants sharing accommodation won't be kitting out the shared areas themselves and are more likely to be looking for the convenience of moving into a furnished space.

There are also many horror stories out there (which have led to HMOs getting a bad rep) whereby bad landlords have been greedy, trying to squeeze too many people into one property. Follow the HMO legislation carefully and act with an ethical business approach, and the advantages will hugely outweigh the drawbacks.

Remember that you may need a licence to operate an HMO and not all properties will qualify. If you are considering an HMO project, ensure that your property will qualify for the licence by contacting the council *before* completing any purchases or refurbishments. Once you have a licence, it will be valid for five years and will come with terms that you must adhere to.

48. YOU MIGHT NEED TO BUY 'OFF PLAN' IN EXPANDING CITIES

In emerging areas where property is in highest demand, you might face buying 'off plan' as the only purchasing option.

Buying off plan means that you commit to purchasing a property before it is actually built. Rather than viewing an existing property, you instead will make your decision based on marketing material.

New build homes are also a form of off plan property, as you view 'show homes' and put your deposit down based on floorplans and marketing material. New builds will be covered in larger detail in Lesson 49, whilst here we focus on cities where off plan is the most common option.

In booming city centres, more and more investors are buying off plan since the areas are such hotspots that properties are snapped up before they are finished. The chances of a new development finishing a project with properties left to sell is unheard of in many cities (take Manchester for example). Even buying off plan is becoming tricky, as investors worldwide are buying one or multiple units before many people have even heard about the building plans.

There are two reasons why you should be extra cautious when buying off plan:

1. Buying off plan is usually necessary in hotspots. See Lesson 36 on why you should avoid hotspots.

2. Buying off plan carries much higher risk than buying a property that is already built. There are always cases whereby investors choose to buy off plan and then experience large delays before they see any ROI. Putting a deposit down on an unbuilt property means you won't get any return for a while, which you could do if you were to invest elsewhere. You need to be sure that this wait will pay off and still be more lucrative than other deals.

However, buying off plan can be beneficial if done correctly. Always follow these five steps:

1. Research the developer just as much as you research the property itself. The developer must be 100% secure. If they go bust, you could lose all your invested money and time.
2. Use a reliable and respectable developer who has a history of completing on time. There's nothing worse than an inexperienced developer running over the proposed schedule, as this is time you should be earning rental profits.
3. Ensure the developer is holding your deposit in escrow or has your deposit insured (if they are using it to fund the project).
4. Look out for great deals that aim to kickstart sales on the project or negotiate better prices right at the start.
5. If you are confident from your THESIS © research that the area will go up in value, buying off plan can be great as you will be purchasing a property for its current market value that will be worth even more when completed.

49. BUY NEW BUILDS AT THE RIGHT TIME

New build properties carry many pros and cons. Let's consider them below:

Advantages of investing in new builds:

- Brand new homes do not require any renovation so can be rented out very quickly (as long as you negotiate the finishing elements to your property as some can be sold even without flooring!).
- Any snags (defects to the property) identified within the first two years of ownership will usually be rectified for free by the development company as per your contract.
- New build homes should adhere to NHBC (National House Building Council) standards. In addition, the property will be covered under the NHBC warranty should anything go wrong.
- New builds are often more attractive to tenants because of their condition and can sometimes attract higher rental yields for that reason.
- They are easy to purchase, as you simply put down a reservation fee on the plot you are interested in and then pay your deposit at a later date.
- For the more advanced investor – some development companies will offer discounts on new build property if multiple plots are purchased at one time.
- The companies who choose where to position the new build developments will have done ample research into the area so you can be sure that it has potential.

Disadvantages of investing in new builds:

- It's much harder to add value to new builds as they are already completed to a high spec and don't accept below market value offers. If you wanted to develop a property to release equity for your next purchase, a new build would not be the best option.
- As the house is brand-spanking new, it can have some teething problems at the start as the house is used and tested for the first time. This can include the walls 'settling' which results in cracks. Whilst these can be easily rectified and repaired for free by the developer, this can be an inconvenience and you would have to rely on your tenants to report them all, especially within the two-year period.
- If you buy at the earlier stage, your property could be part of a construction site for months or even years as the rest of the houses are built around yours. This can cause noise pollution, closed roads and just generally make the property look less appealing.

When is the right time to buy new builds?

The best time to buy new build properties is either in the very early stages of development, or right at the end.

As more and more new builds are constructed on a development, the value of the properties will increase as the location becomes more appealing, so buying right at the start - when the location is less desirable and less people see the area's potential - can be a profitable move. You're also more likely to get a good deal in the very early stages, as the developers are looking to generate as much interest and sales as possible. Buying during the middle of the development phase would mean you would be buying the same property for an elevated price.

Equally, if you purchase at the very end of the construction process, you may be able to get your hands on heavily discounted properties as the developers are keen to get them off their hands and move their sales representatives onto new areas. The last properties to sell on a new build site will be the show homes. This means you could get the added bonus of a fully decorated property for a bargain price. When developers are looking to get rid of the last few properties on a development, they will be more willing to offer great incentives, such as paying towards your stamp duty, offering cashback, or free furnishing upgrades. You will also benefit from moving straight into a completely finished new development.

50. BEWARE OF AUCTIONS

Although auctions used to be a great place to pick up cheap property fast, over recent years they have been glorified by TV programmes (you all know what I'm talking about) who make out the process to be a fool proof, simple, get rich quick strategy. This has led to a false belief that property auctions are an easy way to pick up cheap property to make quick money.

Here's why this is no longer guaranteed:

1. Since the popularity of auction TV shows has risen over the last few years, auctions have been swarmed by first-time investors. Those who have been investing through auction for many years are now declaring that it's more difficult than ever to find a bargain, as novices bid on almost anything, raising the final selling prices on each property.

2. There is always a reason that a property is selling at auction and not through a standard sales agent. Admittedly, the reason can sometimes simply be that the seller requires a quick sale and is willing to achieve a lower selling price. However, more often than not, it is because the property has a serious issue and would not do well on the property market against other competition.

3. There's so much more to do than 'read the legal pack' that the auction TV programmes tell you to do. You must research this property scrupulously. It must be surveyed to assess any damages or required refur-

bishment work and you must secure funding prior to attending the auction. It's all well and good if you have all the capital upfront. But for those who don't, you must be aware of your obligations to pay quickly if you win at auction. This means securing bridging finance [11] before you attend an auction.

4. Most properties at auction will require a significant amount of work to be carried out on them before they can be tenanted. For this reason, many auction bidders are those who are specifically looking to flip property, buying low and then using their resources to add value to the property before selling it on. So, although the property price may appear to be a good deal initially, you must take into consideration not only the required refurbishment costs, but the cost of owning the property without receiving any rental income for the time it takes to get it ready to sell or rent.

If you are interested in buying at auction, always attend at least one 'dummy run' first, to familiarise yourself with the process. This ensures that when you attend with the intention of actually bidding, you already have some experience in the auction room.

Prior to any auction, browse the catalogue and complete a full analysis on any property you are interested in (run numbers to find out what purchase price could equate a good ROI, conduct a THESIS © analysis on the area if you haven't done so already, determine the market value and attend a live or virtual viewing). Before you step into the auction room, you must decide on a maximum price you are prepared to bid, no matter what. You need to be 100% confident of what you are prepared to do in the auction room, before you get there.

After the auction, take the time to re-consider those which failed to sell. Not every property that goes to auction will sell. Perhaps the guide price was considered too high or there were many more appealing properties at that auction. Perhaps turn-out was low on this particular day and there just wasn't any interest. Chances are the seller will still be keen to get rid of the property and might accept a ballsy low offer. If you had already calculated the price you were willing to pay for the property yet it was much lower than the guide price so you didn't bid, there would be no harm in approaching the seller or auction company to put forward your proposal.

51. FLIPPING IS NOT PROPERTY INVESTMENT

There are many property investment TV shows and property investment courses that show flipping properties as a good investment strategy.

However, (although quite a controversial statement that I'm sure not everyone will fully agree with), I believe that flipping property cannot be wholly considered as property investment.

This is not to say that property flipping cannot be a good business strategy, but it is not considered in this book when the terms 'property investment' and 'property investor' are used – we are focusing on buy-to-let!

To talk about property flipping would require an entirely different book and is a very different type of property journey to take.

Let's say I own a shop which sells T-shirts. I buy T-shirts for a wholesale cost from a supplier, add designs to them to increase their value, and then sell them in my shop to the public. This does not make me a T-shirt investor and my business is not T-shirt investing. Rather, it's buying and selling.

Similarly, someone who purchases property to increase its value (either through improvements to the property or simply by buying BMV and selling at market value) is not a property investor. They operate in the property market, but they are not making investments. They are buying and selling.

Let's look at some differentiations:

- The goal of a property flipper is to generate cash through the buying and selling of property.
- The goal of a property investor is to build a portfolio of profitable properties in order to generate an income each month whilst holding onto them over the long-term.

- A property flipper will purchase and sell property quickly, during one phase of the property cycle. They will be looking to sell it on for a profit as quickly as possible, before the market changes.
- A property investor builds a portfolio of properties over-time through many property cycles, which they hold onto for as long as it is financially intelligent to do so. They only release assets if selling could open up a better opportunity for a different investment.

- A property flipper will look to add value twice (buying below market value and renovation work) as quickly as possible.
- A property investor will look to add value THRICE (buying below market value, renovation work and through capital growth).

- A property flipper is interested in net profits.
- A property investor is interested in yields and ROIs.

- A property flipper is only interested in instant gratification.
- A property investor is interested in deferred gratification (but will also achieve instant gratification through rental income).

- A property flipper will use leverage by way of bridging finance (short-term, high interest loans) or will purchase outright using cash.

- A property investor will use leverage by taking good debt (mortgages) to fund the purchase.

I'm sure there will be investors out there who may disagree and think that flipping *is* a property investment strategy. This is quite natural as the lines between buying and selling and investing are slightly blurred in the centre. Yet within this book we will consider property investing as purchasing and holding onto property for the mid to long-term.

PHASE THREE: PURCHASING PROPERTY

CHAPTER 9:
FINANCING

52. BANKS LEND CAPITAL FOR PROPERTY BASED ON 'LOAN TO VALUE' (LTV)

Loan to value (LTV) is the amount of capital that a lender is willing to let you borrow in the form of a mortgage, expressed as a percentage, compared to the value of the property. It is essentially a percentage of the total value of the property at the time of purchase, with your deposit making up the remainder.

For buy-to-let properties, a standard mortgage would generally offer a 75% LTV, meaning a 25% deposit is required. Having to pay a quarter of the property value upfront is perhaps one of the reasons why moderately priced terraced houses are the most common type of rental property an investor will look to purchase. This is because coming up with 25% of the value of a more expensive detached house is quite a stretch and it is better to own two small properties over one big one [57].

Depending on market conditions, some lenders might offer more favourable LTVs to different individuals (depending on their situation, credit score, etc.) Some lenders do offer 80% LTV for buy-to-let properties. However, larger LTVs often come with higher interest rates to reflect the increased level of risk lenders are taking. Although almost unheard of for investors,

90% and 95% mortgages do exist but are usually reserved exclusively for first-time residential buyers.

When comparing buy-to-let mortgages, it can be easy to assume that the highest LTV on offer is the best deal since it allows for the lowest possible down payment (deposit). It's true that the less capital needed upfront, the quicker you can obtain a property. But don't forget that this would mean that the repayments each month would be higher as you take on more debt and the value of interest charged would also be higher.

When looking into your mortgage choices, speak with your broker and consider all options carefully. Run the numbers on each choice before selecting the one that's best for you and your specific situation.

53. A BUY-TO-LET MORTGAGE ISN'T YOUR ONLY OPTION

A buy-to-let mortgage is the most common way to finance a rental property. Yet it certainly isn't the only funding option available to you. There are several alternative financing methods which are increasing in popularity. When embarking on your property journey, consider these funding alternatives carefully to help you set your strategies.

Beginner:

- **Lease Option:** Essentially, you pay the property owner an agreed sum of money each month which allows you to manage and rent the property (the 'lease'). At a later, fixed date, you can purchase the property from the owner if you want to (the 'option'), at a price you agreed on at the start of your lease. If you choose not to purchase the property, you simply hand it back to the owner. It offers the opportunity to 'try before you buy'. Using a lease option means that you don't need a hefty deposit as you would with a buy-to-let mortgage – just the 'consideration' fee which can be as low as £1! As you agree the purchase price in advance, if the property market goes up, you can instantly add value to your purchase by getting it BMV at the time of purchase.

Intermediate:

- **Peer to Peer lending:** This is covered in Lesson 11.

-     **Crowdfunding:** A financing strategy whereby a group of people each contribute capital towards the purchase of a property. The investors can choose to put in as much or as little as they want, and each property can be owned by as many investors as is necessary to reach 100% of the required funds. The contributors will each own a part of the property (which will be set up as a company by the crowdfunding agency) – and will receive profits from that company relative to their contribution. Crowdfunding can be as simple as four people each investing 25% capital into a property purchase, and can get as complicated as 'development crowdfunding' whereby dozens of investors each contribute a tiny percentage into a share of a development project such as a block of flats or row of new houses.

Before proceeding with any of the above buy-to-let mortgage alternatives, it is fundamental that you seek out your own in-depth research or speak with a professional broker.

54. CONSIDER JOINT VENTURES – BUT BE CAREFUL WHO YOU WORK WITH

Joint ventures (JVs) consist of teaming up with another person/other people to work on an investment together. JVs are common with people who already know each other. Friends, family members and colleagues are the most common types of people to collaborate on JVs.

JVs are great for combining skills and shouldn't be considered solely for financial reasons. Perhaps you are great at numbers and have a good property education, but you aren't as good when it comes to hands-on work. Teaming up with someone who shares the same goals but has a different skill set could benefit both sides by using different areas of expertise to create a team that are stronger together.

Yet, who you choose to embark on a JV with should be considered extremely carefully. It is commonly said that you shouldn't mix business with people from your personal life. This is because money can cause strained relationships and test friendships.

In order to minimise any issues during a JV, it is strongly advised to create a script in which each party agrees the steps that will be taken and the terms that will be followed in advance. Even when working with someone you have known for years and are extremely close to, the script will ensure that your relationship is maintained and that the process remains uncomplicated. By ironing out as many decisions as possible before the investing starts, you will be able to test your JV relationship (which will differ to your personal or working relationship) before investing a penny.

What your 'script' should include:

- A financial statement related to each person involved. This should include credit scores, income, monthly savings, etc. to prove that each person is eligible for lending and in a position to deal with the financial requirements of the investment. Note that if you invest with someone, your credit score can be affected by theirs.
- A detailed list of all expected costs. How and when they will be paid, and by whom.
- Account details for where money will be deposited for the JV and where all income will go into, plus who will have access to it and when.
- Details of who will contribute in exactly what way.
- Time frames for each task.
- Risk management [83] – How to react to worst case scenarios.
- How to exit the JV if one or all parties want to leave the agreement.
- What will be done in the case of non-compliance.
- The percentage of contribution each person is making, comparable to the percentage of the returns they will receive.

The script should be as detailed as possible, right down to who will clean the property and put the bins out during a void period. The more information the script includes before you start the JV, the easier the process, and the better your relationship will be when you complete the investment and come out on the other side.

55. DO YOUR RESEARCH BEFORE CHOOSING A FIXED OR VARIABLE RATE MORTGAGE

When buying a property using a mortgage, you will need to choose whether to opt for a fixed or variable rate.

A fixed rate mortgage will mean that the percentage of interest you pay on the loan is fixed each month for a set period of time (usually 2 or 5 years), regardless of what happens to interest rates.

Fixed rates are good as they guarantee what your repayments will be each month, making it easier to budget and calculate accurate ROIs and net yields[24]. However, the rates can be slightly higher than variable rate mortgages and you won't be able to benefit from lower interest rates should the base rate drop.

With variable rate mortgages, the interest charged on the mortgage can go up or down depending on the base rate set by the Bank of England [58].

Variable rates can fall into three categories, and each can be capped or uncapped. A cap on interest means that there's a limit on the maximum level of interest you can be charged.

1. **Tracker mortgages**: The rate is tracked on a fixed economic indicator, which is the Bank of England's official borrowing rate (also known as the base rate) [58]. It will not be exactly the same as the base rate, but it will move up and down in line with it.
2. **Standard Variable Rate mortgages (SVRs)**: These rates are determined by each lender and can vary away from the base rate. They are less desirable than trackers or fixed rate mortgages and will be what you end up on if your agreed mortgage term expires and you don't remortgage onto a better deal. The benefit of SVR mortgages is that they don't usually have re-payment charges. Therefore, you can choose to pay off your mortgage quicker or switch to a new mortgage deal without incurring any penalty charges.
3. **Discount Rate mortgages**: These are deals whereby lenders apply an initial discount to their SVRs. These can offer some of the lowest deals on the market but may only be available for part of your mortgage term. For example, a six-month discounted SVR within a two-year contract.

It can be difficult to determine whether the base rate will go up or down. As a result of this, investors generally feel safer on a fixed rate, despite the fact that interest rates are slightly higher. As a result, they don't have to worry about the economy taking a turn for the worse.

On a variable rate, investors can enjoy the benefits of a lower interest rate compared to those offered on fixed-rates. As long as investors have planned out all the scenarios and stress tested their investments, they are able to maximise their ROI with the savings from the lower interest rates.

The good news is that interest rates won't change overnight, so if the economy were to show signs of taking a turn for the worse, there would be time to re-assess investments to determine whether it might be worth remortgaging onto a fixed rate at the end of the mortgage term.

To decide if a fixed or variable rate would be best for your investment, you need to do lots of research. Most importantly, consider the state of the economy and anticipate how it may fluctuate over the proposed term of your mortgage. Take a look at how interest rates have moved over recent years and evaluate where abouts the property market is in the 18-year property cycle. Speak to your broker and network with other investors to see what mortgages they are opting for right now.

56. INTEREST ONLY MORTGAGES ARE USUALLY MUCH BETTER THAN REPAYMENT MORTGAGES

When choosing the right mortgage for your investment, you will need to choose whether to take on a repayment or interest only mortgage.

Repayment mortgages are the most common form of mortgage type for homeowners. People have been conditioned to believe that they should get a good education so they can get a good job, buy a big house to live in and pay off their mortgage as soon as possible.

Repayment mortgages are suitable for those who wish to reduce their mortgage debt overtime, by paying back a fraction of it, plus interest, each month over a number of years (usually between around 25 and 35).

Interest only mortgages are those whereby the owner of the debt pays the interest of said debt off each month but does not pay off any of the original debt. This means that the debt taken out does not reduce overtime, and at the end of the fixed term, the debt owed will still be the same.

There are three reasons why interest only mortgages are usually the best option for investors:

1. First and foremost, due to inflation, interest only mortgages cause the debt to depreciate in 'real time' value over time. This means that rather than working hard now to pay off a repayment mortgage, it is better to let the debt sit for a while and become less valuable. When the debt is worth less, it will be much easier to pay off quickly. Leverage is incredibly important and will be covered in much greater detail in the next tip.

2. Secondly, by paying interest only, rental profits will be higher each month. This allows investors to save quicker to reinvest in additional investments, thus increasing their net worth.

3. Finally, many interest-only mortgages come with the option to make additional repayments if you want to. So, if you decide you want to pay off some of the debt for whatever reason, you usually can.

57. IT'S BETTER TO BUY TWO SMALL PROPERTIES THAN ONE BIG ONE: LEVERAGE

Leverage is an investment strategy of using borrowed money to finance the purchase of an asset and increase the potential return of an investment.

Leverage is a form of good debt [8] as it enables you to take on property investments that generate returns whilst they also increase in value overtime.

Many people who don't possess a property education dedicate their 9-5 savings to paying off the mortgage on their home as quickly as possible. Yet, being open to good debt and using leverage is the most beneficial action for yielding large returns.

Property investors use leverage as it allows them to purchase property much faster than if they had to come up with 100% of the property value themselves – which could take decades for many people!

It is also used by those who may already have enough to buy one property yet invest in multiple properties with the same amount of capital, since using leverage to purchase several properties is more lucrative than purchasing one outright.

Let's consider some simple numbers to illustrate this. Although this will not go as far as to detail all costs involved, such as stamp duty and agency fees, the example purely exists to demonstrate the power of leverage.

Scenario:

Let's say you have access to £100,000 to invest in property. You could choose to purchase one £97,000 property outright, plus £3,000 legal fees (Option 1), or use the same £100,000 to pay deposits on FIVE £70,000 properties (5 X £17,500 for the deposits and £12,500 total on legal fees) by taking a 75% LTV mortgage (£52,000) on each of them on a fixed, 2% interest only deal (Option 2).

Potential Outcomes:

	Monthly Income (rent)	Monthly Outgoing (mortgage)	Annual Profit
Option 1	£800	0	(£800 - £0) X 12 = £9,600
Option 2	£650 X 5 = £3,250	£90 X 5 = £450	(£3,250 - £450) X 12 = £33,600

Now let's consider that we have purchased the properties in locations which have been well researched and after 2-3 years the values of all properties in each option have increased by a modest 10%. My sole property in Option 1 would now be worth £106,700 (a gain of £9,700), whereas my property portfolio in Option 2 would be worth £385,000 (a gain of £35,000).

Thinking even further ahead, after one decade (considering that properties double in value on average every 9 years), the property in Option 1 could have doubled to £194,000. The combined value of the five properties in Option 2 could have doubled to £700,000! That's enough capital gain to pay off each of the five £52,000 mortgages and have £440,000 left over (before costs and taxes due).

To reiterate, this is an extremely simplified example. It does not take into consideration specific costs or taxes which are covered in other lessons, but it should help you to understand the incredible power of leverage.

58. KEEP TRACK OF INTEREST RATES

To succeed in property investment, it is crucial to understand how interest rates work and to constantly keep an eye on them. Investing without consideration for interest rates can dramatically affect your investment portfolio and even cause you to go into negative equity and fail as an investor.

Here is a breakdown of the 10 most important things to know about interest rates:

1. **Interest rates are set by The Bank of England.** This is called the 'bank rate' also referred to as the 'base rate' and it acts as a sort of guideline for other financial institutions.

2. **Interest rates are adjusted to suit the needs of the economy.** Interest rates fluctuate in line with the performance of the economy. This includes lowering rates to help stabilise the economy in times of hardship (such as implications caused by Brexit) and increasing rates when demand for lending rises.

3. **Interest is charged on borrowing and earned on savings.** When you borrow money, interest is the cost paid to the lender in exchange for lending that amount. This is often expressed as Annual Percentage Rate (APR) and takes into account the interest rate and charges. When you save money in the bank, you earn interest. Depending on the type of account it can be subject to different terms and conditions (e.g. the account holder must leave the money in the

bank for a set period of time or deposit a set amount each month).

4. **Interest rates for lending vary according to risk.** Once the Bank of England has set the base rate, lenders will set their own rates for lending depending on risk. Therefore, interest rates on riskier things such as interest only loans and high LTVs will be higher. Buy-to-let mortgages are considered to carry more risk than residential mortgages which is why they also carry higher interest rates.

5. **Using leverage (and paying interest) is more lucrative than saving money in a bank and receiving interest.** When interest rates are low, it costs you less to borrow money. This also means you earn less on your savings. As inflation is normally higher than the interest you can earn from the bank, your money sat in the bank is not earning enough to keep up with inflation [57].

6. **Profits and ROI depend on interest rates.** Interest rates count as a 'cost', so the amount is deducted from your income. Since interest rates are always changing, it is essential to stress test [40]. Whilst current figures might seem appealing, we need to be certain that should the market change, your investments will still be safe enough to weather through any tougher times where higher interest rates are being charged.

7. **You can get fixed or variable interest rates for mortgages** [55].

8. **Interest rates have been very attractive for the last 10-12 years**[25]. In March 2020 the base rate was lowered to 0.10% which is the lowest ever rate! It has been below 2% since January 2009 (lowered to stabilise the economy following the last market crash). The highest interest rate on record was 14.88% in

our divorce settlement substantial enough to cover Rachel's tuition at her dream school, UCSB, and her sorority expenses, but it also provided me with enough resources to reclaim my life.

Isn't it remarkable? God works in mysterious ways to demonstrate His infinite love and ensure we are never forsaken. His hand guides us through trials and tribulations, turning moments of despair into triumphs, reminding us that even the most difficult situations can lead to greater blessings. And that, dear reader, is the incredible journey of faith that continues to unfold in my life.

www.ingramcontent.com/pod-product-compliance
Ingram Content Group UK Ltd.
Pitfield, Milton Keynes, MK11 3LW, UK
UKHW030648130225
455042UK00012B/72/J

9 798891 240568